Praise for E

M000209729

WHEN COWS WORE SHOES

"Engaging, delightful and full of personality! EP Rose writes of her family summers living in the small rural village of Ruesga, Spain. Rose's photographic diary of family and village life add captivating and touching visuals throughout her adventurous tale of loving friendships, joyous simplicity and life changing events. "

— debra Reingold Reiss, photojournalist

"...more than a pastoral, idyllic romance... When Cows Wore Shoes is a sensitive portrait in words and photos of hardship, poverty, loss, and longing of a time and place lost to history...Felicidades! to the author and her young sons who embraced the joy of rural living and the welcoming company of villagers who would become family."

—Barbara Strelke, author of
Franco is Dead! Viva España! and *Journey Home Times Four*

"In this excellent memoir, E. P. Rose has written a colorful tale that takes the reader back to a rural lifestyle that has all but vanished. A life-long city dweller, I found myself drawn into her colorful story of ancient farming, its people, traditions and culture intriguing. The author's keen and loving eye showed me a little of the magic she experienced each summer in the tiny Spanish village of Ruesga."

—Ellen Dupuy, broadcaster, journalist

"With a crackling wit and an eloquent vulnerability, Rose has a knack for finding the perfect anecdote to porty a certain time and place – and the emotional lives of those living through it. At turns touching, funny, insightful, and profound, When Cows Wore Shoes is an excellent read."

—Jeff Deutsch, author of
In Praise Of Good Bookstores, Princeton University Press

WHEN COWS WORE SHOES

E.P. Rose

E.P. ROSE

First Edition

Studio on 41 Press
Galisteo, New Mexico
galisteoliz.com

Printed in the U.S.A.

ISBN: 978-0-9861188-7-6

This book is intended to provide accurate information with regard to the subject matter covered. However, the author and publisher accept no responsibility for inaccuracies or omissions.

Book design by Donna Brownell

Title page impression: cylinder seal, Arslantepe-Malatya, Turkey, depicting a ritual thresh, dated to the third millennium BC

Cover photo by Kate Jefferson

Photos and drawings from the family albums of the author and her son, Anthony Jefferson.

to the beauty of living simply and to the people of ruesga.

Juan

Mercedes

Juanillo

Aquilino

Angel

El Cazador

Ulpiano and Juanna

Mariano and Manuella

Alejandro

Leandero

Miles, Ed, Anthony

Liz

the Anton family: La Madre, Ignacio, Alejandro, Ulpiano, Manuella

PROLOGUE

"Shoes? Cow shoes?" Friends usually giggle and look at me sideways when I tell them the cows wore shoes and worked in the fields.

"Like leather booties, do you mean?" They would ask puzzled, "but not cows. Surely you must mean oxen?" And I would shake my head, remembering.

"No, I mean milking cows. All the villagers own working cows. They couldn't survive without them," I attempted to explain. "Plough, thresh, and collect the grain, they need the cows for just about everything," my voice trailed.

I saw the gentle beasts in my mind. Breathed in their sweet grass breath. Heard the soft clonk of their bells and the hiss of our friend's sledges gliding over his harvested grain. Yoked together, they worked in pairs plodding contentedly pulling an empty or heavily laden wooden cart to and from the village fields. *Estrella, La Machina,*

Romera, Princessa. Recalling the cows' names, I smiled.

"Cows wearing shoes was not so odd really once you realize how the villagers' survival depended on them," I concluded my explanation.

I picked up the iron cow shoe I kept on my desk as a paperweight, and holding it in my hand ran my fingers along its outer curve. Shaped a little like a human ear pierced by five nail holes, I found its shape beautiful. A nostalgic reminder of our Spanish summers in Ruesga, and my son's and my surprise when we discovered cows wore shoes.

One day our first summer, exploring to see where a narrow lane would take us, my sons, and I came across a curious sight in the corner of a field of a cow suspended from a four-poster bed-like frame by a wide leather strap cinched beneath her belly. One leg bent, and propped on a low stump. The man with her appeared to be hammering something to the cow's hoof

"That's Nestor with her. What's he doing to that poor cow, Mum? *Holá.* Nestor," Miles called running towards him.

Unable to speak for the nails held between his teeth, Nestor looked up and beckoned us closer. Removing one nail at a time, he anchored a curious-shaped iron shoe over half the under surface of her hoof followed by a second to mirror the second. Of course. Cows' hooves are cleft, I explained to myself.

"See, Anthony and Miles? Two shoes per hoof. Eight shoes in all."

"*Càlmate, Bella. Casi. Casi,*" Nearly done, Nestor soothed calling her by name.

Then shaving the horn of each half till they matched, he was done.

"*Esta, Bella,*" Nestor patted Bella's neck, and loosening the belt let her drop allowing her to stand and gallop into the field.

As Nestor tossed Bella's damaged shoe into the pile of discards, the boys rushed to retrieve it.

"Is it alright if we each have one?" They gestured.

"*Si. Si. Toma,*" he assented with a wave of his hand. *Tontos.* Weird foreigners, I could practically hear him thinking.

I lived for those summers we spent in Spain. Dreamed ten

months for that day in July when Ed's university and Anthony and Miles' school closed for the year, for packing to be over, and blackened pots and pans, camping paraphernalia and sleeping bags gathered and loaded into the mini and we could drive away.

Stifling London suburbia, was no place for four-year-old Miles and Anthony, my deaf six-year-old son, to spend their two-month school holidays. More importantly I wanted my children to experience another culture and not have them growing up believing the only correct way to live was the British way and that success equated money.

No, I wanted a magical childhood for my boys, for them to run feral, roam the unseen worlds of their imagination as I had on Devon's heather moors.

I had my chance. Now it was their turn. Before formal dos and don'ts forever cemented my children into a British mold.

The story I want to tell is of a Spanish people living in a slow-paced village high in the Picos de Europa, when cows wore shoes, and men and women had no use for banknotes, machines or cars. It was a gentle way of life that is no more when time slowed so still my thoughts evaporated.

Sometimes real, sometimes imagined, the stories weave a portrait of the village people I knew and loved over eleven summers. I had no idea at the time the eleventh would be our last, when with no goodbyes, no explanation, we suffocated the fire-pit with river-stones, bundled our tents and blackened kettle into our mini and combed the flattened grass upright. All trace of our summers erased, we drove away from our Spanish friends never to return.

Even now more than fifty years later, the word Spain conjures the crinkled faces of our Ruesgan friends working fields of sunlit grain, the sweet smell of cow patties spattered in the lane, and the gentle clonk of cowbells from wooden carts creaking past the Juanon. How could I forget? Those memories... the soughing hiss of threshing sledges gliding seas of golden grain ride in my veins. I cannot imagine who I'd be without those eleven summers connected to the earth in Ruesga that changed the direction of my life. There in that rural village, I learned to loosen my British straitjacket and slip back into my own skin.

1

HOW IT ALL BEGAN

Perhaps in Spain…

Here, I said pointing to a dot in the Spanish Mountains after hours of sprawling over a map spread on the living room floor. And so Ruesga, a tiny mountain village high in the Picos de Europa became the place we chose to uncover the mysterious society hidden within the random spot I marked, where I discovered cows wore shoes, and small was beautiful.

The Spanish Cross Channel Ferry sailed for Bilbao in one week. I was excited to spend our first holiday together as a family. Ed had moved in with me a year back: to be my life partner, and step-father to my boys, I hoped cautiously. But that was before. Before I understood Ed was not the partner for me.

At the very time we should be leaving to catch the Plymouth-Bilbao ferry, he banged the front door shut and without a word was gone. Disappeared. Nowhere to be found, leaving the boys and me frantically tidying and cleaning my London house for holiday renters —money I needed for my three fares to Spain.

"Can you help?" I pleaded, pounding my neighbors' door.

It took them an agonizing hour to locate and coax him home from a local London pub, and manhandle him into our already packed and overloaded mini. I glanced at Ed. Eyes closed, his head lolled against the window. Drained of strength, I'd not the courage to question him and risk his rage.

"Don't worry, darlings. We'll make it okay," I reassured my two wide-eyed boys. "Just go to sleep, and by the time you wake up we'll be there."

Safely curled up together on the back seat, they nodded but didn't say a word.

Evening had turned to night. I released my foot from the clutch pedal, pressed the accelerator and we finally set off. Once the last of the city lights faded behind us, I checked my watch. Five to six hour's drive to reach the port of Plymouth. Pale and exhausted, white-knuckled, I gripped the wheel peering into the darkness ahead.

A line of angry tears wet my cheeks and I wept a little from pure tension. Then at last, night lifted and the first watery rays of dawn revealed the day as I cruised between the port's gates and onto the ferry.

"Oh. Are we there already?" Ed asked cheerfully, the evening's drama clearly forgotten.

I hate ships, the smell of engine oil, I dread the thirty-six hours at sea I'd have to endure trapped below deck flat on my bunk. Eyes closed, my guts rising and dropping with the ship's pitch and roil, we steamed our way across the English Channel and through the infamous Bay of Biscay wishing I were dead.

"Thank goodness that's over," I exclaimed when the ship's engines cut, stopped its rocking, and my feet finally touched land.

"Are you alright now Mummy?" Anthony and Miles asked in unison, sliding their hands into mine.

I looked over at Ed. No sign of a hangover, no mention of remorse, he looked at me and smiled.

"Yes, my darlings. Now we're here, I'm just fine." I squeezed their hands.

"Looks like a five-hour drive from the map. You ready boys? Then let's get the hell out of this ugly place," Ed called out with a wave at Bilbao's jungle of metal derricks and cranes.

Piled back in the mini, Ed floored it to put as many miles as quickly as he could between us and Bilbao's grimy factories. The sulphuric smell of pollution cleared, the suburbs thinned, and the city's grey outline faded behind us. We wound down the car windows and breathed in the country air. Look. Look. We exclaimed unable to believe the paradise surrounding us.

Red-roofed houses, the postcard villages and the greenest emerald hills dotted with black and white Friesians cows grazing peacefully on its idyllic pastures, the sparkling streams catching the sun, the bluer-than-blue, blue sky. I looked again at the rivulets of water cascading to the valleys. Livid green, one ran red, every stream completely polluted.

"Ooofff." I stared open mouthed. "Those cows, they're eating poisoned grass. No way we're drinking milk from around here."

Turning East away from the coast, a couple of kilometers later, enticing, partly veiled in mist, a distant range of mountains emerged from the layer of cloud at its feet triggering a memory of Everest I'd seen as a child.

I was six, Anthony's age.

"Never forget," my father commanded. "You've seen the highest mountain in the world." And the image and wonder of those white sails skimming the sea-blue sky has stayed.

"Anthony, Miles. Look boys," I exclaimed wishing them the same child's magic. "That's where we're going. Up over those mountains above the clouds."

I leaned back in my seat and daydreamed my way to the village we sped towards. Inching the twisting road up towards the pass, then down the other side through mountain meadows and fields of hay. The scattering of cottages gave way to villages complete with ancient churches and shday plazas. I was amazed to see a couple of larger towns still clustered around pillared squares that had stood there since Roman times.

"REINOSA, AGUILAR DE CAMPO," I read their names out loud. "CERVERA DE PISUERGA, the final town. Just a few more miles to go. Look."

RUESGA. 4 kilometers.

The mini slowed, nosed into a stretch of paved roadway that dead-ended in a dot on the map and swung suddenly right beneath an almost vertical hillside that seemed in danger of tumbling into our path. To our left, a patchwork of hay and still-green standing field of corn, to a curving line of poplars where we guessed a river flowed.

Rounding the final bend, there stood the village. No village could be more perfectly dreamt up; a church, a winding lane, a row of stone houses, the slope of curved red clay roofs, each stone, each tile, tightly gripped in place like pieces of a jigsaw. To complete the picture, a cluster of poplar trees cradled a sun-dappled pool of a river. Treacle slow, the Rio Pisuerga's water slid beneath the arc of a stone bridge. Wanting to cry, I burst out laughing instead. As we crossed over the mighty divide of the bridge into the sunlit village on the far side, I had the clear feeling I had penetrated the Curtain wall of a Castle Keep, and been granted entry into the magical unknown of the future.

I was right to feel as I did. We all four of us lost our edges and became gentler, more rounded people. The boys, me and Ed, absorbed more knowledge from those eleven summers in Spain than any of us could ever have imagined.

A lone man, the man I later knew to be Alejandro, stood below the bridge at the edge of the shallow ford watering a pair of cows. Yoked together, knee-deep in the river, chins dripping, curious, both cows and man, raised their heads and fixedly observed our entry. I saw no other living thing. Not a person, animal or bird.

"Gosh. It's mid-afternoon. Strange to be so empty," we remarked not yet understanding the local custom of siesta.

Facing inwards to hidden courtyards, the deserted lane wound out of sight between a row of stone houses. But for the flare of red geraniums sprouting from tin cans on many of the window sills, the granite facades and closed doors, we might have got the impression we were not welcome. Instead, I felt the buildings wrap around us. Protective. Safe.

"Ruesga. Ruesga," I called out. "The end of the road. We've arrived." I double-checked the map as Ed slowed to a stop in front of the only bar.

A one-word sign. "*CUARTOS*. Rooms," I translated from my phrasebook and took a deep breath.

"This is it everybody." No shops, no square, no café, we pulled up outside a modern building attached to the bar. The only one of its kind, and the tallest in the village, its yellow edifice rose nakedly alien among the village's century's old two-story buildings.

2

THE BAR JUANON

Was I crazy? Had I made a terrible mistake coming to this isolated place? Beyond *'Buenas dias, si, non'* and *'gracias'* neither of us spoke a word of Spanish. How on earth to get by? What if people were unfriendly? Oh well, too late to turn back now. Forcing a smile, I opened the door and stepped out onto the hard-packed earth rubbing the stiffness from my lower back.

Wiping hands on her blue-flowered apron, a stout, dark-haired woman in the doorway, froze in place before walking firmly towards us. Motherly, was my first impression of her, and kind, her body language and features declared. I immediately cheered. Perhaps she felt the same of me, for she held out her arms.

"Bienvenidos," she smiled. *"Soy Mercedes."*

Taking both her hands, I smiled right back. *"Me llama Isabel. Ed.*

Tonio. Milo," I pointed to each.

"Encantanda," She ruffled the hair of both boys and bent to give each a hug. *"Holá Tonio. Holá Milo."*

"Ven." She beckoned us to follow her inside the gloomy bar and up the dark flight of stairs to two rooms in the modern part of the building. A matrimonio for Ed and me, and the other with two single beds for the boys.

Shuttered. Dark. Adequate. Not exactly inviting. No furniture apart from the bed, a lone faux wood-grained chipboard wardrobe loomed from a corner on the green lino floor. Disappointed, I took in the stark space, swallowed and forced a nod. I saw no chair, no table, no rug, no place for Ed's typewriter, our books, my pads of drawing paper and box of paints. And we'd planned to fill our days writing, sketching and reading.

In the slightly awkward silence, Mercedes walked over to the window and with a push of the shutters a burst of champagne air, blinding sunlight and the sweet tang of farm-animal smells flooded the stark room totally transforming it.

"Ah. Si. Si," I gasped involuntarily moving to stand beside her.

Framed by the window, spread a pastoral scene of perfection. Up, down, whichever way I turned I saw only tranquility compressed beneath a multicolored colored hillside of strip fields streaked with yellowing grain. Following the curve of the earth lane below us, the lane lead between two rows of houses and past the church all the way back to the hump-backed bridge we crossed a few moments before.

"Look. Even a stork's nest," I exclaimed pointing to the higgly-piggly crown of twigs piled on a corner of the village church tower. "They're supposed to bring good luck," I laughed happily squeezing both boys to me. "Listen. Cow bells. Do you hear?"

Leaning over the sill as far as we could came a rhythmic *Chunk-ker-chink*, as a bow-legged elderly woman appeared from the opposite direction herding a cow and its calf towards the river.

"Look Mum, she's got boats on her feet," Miles exclaimed pointing to her wooden clogs.

Not the tinkling I imagined from cowbells, *Chink-kerchink*, the sound came again from a wooden bell swinging from a wide leather strap cinched round the mother cow's neck. As mother and calf passed its gentle note sounded again with each step, and I froze mid-breath for fear the centuries old scene should vanish.

"*Si. Si. Here, perfecto, senora,*" I smiled clasping my hands in delight, and forcing myself to the present. I flicked through my phrase book. "*Necisita un silla y una mesa por favor.*"

Though we didn't know it then, that first summer was to be one of the three we lived above the Bar Juanon as paying guests of Mercedes. Ridiculously affordable even to us, all in, accommodation for the four of us, food and wine included for less than three quid a day, Ed and I exchanged glances hardly believing our luck.

This would be a real holiday…no cooking, no chores, surrounded by only Castilian Spanish speakers we'd experience first-hand how a Spanish family lived.

There we were, dropped into rural Spain in a tiny village barely marked on a map with the chance to briefly glimpse how people lived in the historical past.

Two months living by the sun like the animals, birds and the village people, was too good an opportunity to miss, we agreed.

"Here goes." Ed announced unbuckling his watchstrap and kissing his wrist. "To nature's clock."

It took Mercedes a flustered few days before a small table and a chair appeared—rustled from a family village kitchen, I learned later to my shame. And all for what, the half dozen pages Ed squeezed from the typewriter? The couple of chapters I forced myself to read?

"Our books are superfluous, here," we concluded. "Our paints, the typewriter too."

Except for our bi-lingual dictionary and Berlitz phrase book Ed's typewriter, our books, paper, paints and brushes remained untouched that summer.

Thank goodness they did, for it was then, that summer in Spain, the first time in my life, I became aware of daylight's gentle glide to night and the intense silence suspended within its blue-black shadows. Sitting on the wall, I witnessed my first moonrise, and tracked the Evening Star float its way to heaven.

Contentment came to me that summer sitting on that wall doing not anything at all. A hard lesson for me to learn, I learned the art of *mañana.*

"Fretting changes not a thing," I tell myself nowadays.

"What is, is what is."

In a traffic queue, a doctor's waiting room, railway station, airport, or leading an elderly person across a street, I repeat the mantra.

3

OUR VERY FIRST YEAR

Make-believe of course, we cheated. No choice. Outsiders, Ed and I knew it was impossible to live as the villagers, particularly our first year. Unlike them, we didn't have to work to eat. Hard currency jingled in our pockets and we had the luxury of paying for our food and a place to sleep. We quickly found out not one person had ever heard of anyone from over the water, let alone England, so finding us suddenly embedded in their midst it was no wonder we were viewed as a curiosity. It didn't take too many days to accept us as harmless.

"*Ingleses*, you know, are sun-worshipers from across the water." We heard Alejandro proudly inform his friends in the bar one evening later after he got to know Ed.

That first year in the late sixties, 1969, the year before the currency exchange rocketed in our favor and plummeted the value of the

Spanish *peseta*, was one of only three summers we lived under a roof not made of canvas. British sterling rose so strong we could afford to lodge at the Juanon. No cleaning, no cooking, no housekeeping chores, four people, two rooms, full board, all meals including a bottle of wine, and another of *gaseosa*, a local sweet drink for the children; the cost—two pounds and fifty pence, about five dollars a day. Too good to be true, we jumped at the chance.

Regularly, from one to two or even three o'clock some days, we, the strange foreigners became a fixture perched there in a row on that wall outside the Juanon waiting for the call to lunch. An oddity to be stared at, It took a week or two, but little by little people smiled and nodded as they passed.

The perfect opportunity for us to people-watch, we too began to recognize certain individuals, distinguish the cows, even, by their unique patterned coloring, the tones of cow's bell, the creak of carts they pulled, and the men that walked behind them and how they trod the earth. Rather than from their facial features, we got to tell the women apart from the unique shapes and shades of the woven willow baskets they carried to the meadow and returned laden down with freshly dug vegetables for the family *comida*. More fun than I-spy, we got into our guessing game. Even the calls of roosters sounded different if we listened carefully and could identify whose courtyards they came from. The more we looked, the more still we remained, the more village lifted its skirts to us exposing a glimmer of its cultural petticoats. And all without us having to take a single step.

Comida, the main meal of the day, appeared when it appeared. Spanish time. One, two or three thirty, when didn't matter. *Depende,* the Spanish shrugged.

Clock-watching and starving, we sat on the low wall outside the Juanon waiting till Mercedes called us to the table. Accustomed as I was to punctual, regular and earlier mealtimes, the not knowing, the indeterminate wait and gnawing hunger made me grumpy and impatient.

"Where the hell is lunch? Look at the time. Do you think she's forgotten?" I grumbled checking and re-checking the sun's position for the umpteenth time. I swung my legs against the wall. Kicked it furiously.

"For God's sake re-lax," Ed reproved, tossing me a packet of *pipas* to keep me going. "We're in Spain on Spanish time."

But I was a doer, a person who'd been taught to sit down during the day was sinful. It took me three interminable weeks of distress and time-watching that first summer before I calmed and accepted lunch would come when it would come. Three weeks before I learned to turn my face to the sun and still my mind. Surprise, surprise, I discovered patience.

Many days while we sat waiting, a blind man tapped his way to the wall and sit with us. Angel was his name. Some days he arrived before us, sometimes after.

"Buen dia," he always greeted sensing our presence. Not looking in our direction, he faced straight ahead.

"Buen dia, Senor Angel," the four of us chorused in reply.

Sightless, smooth-cheeked despite his age, a white cane between his knees, back straight, formally dressed in navy jacket and tie, the old man sat content, face to the sky, noting, seeing everything around him. Did he feel my eyes upon him, the boldness of my stare, the wonder I felt at his calm? If so, his body language, and facial expression never changed.

I tipped my face to the sun like him, and from behind closed lids saw what the blind man saw; the steady pad of passing cows, the creaking of the carts they pulled, and gentle ring of the bells about their necks, some wooden, some iron. Then from the church tower came the clack of a storks' bill and the answering clack from his mate, and pictured the mated pair rising from their nest, flapping their wings and rubbing beaks. I learned to distinguish the light tread of a woman from the clop of a man. Warm rays burnished my cheek, my arms and legs. I inhaled. I breathed till my mind lay quiet and my mind became as an empty vessel. I smiled at the simplicity of my discovery. At the peace I felt, and the dreams I dreamed.

Just being in the village and adapting to the slow pace and the unusual pleasure of doing nothing was enough. No timetable for work or meals. No hurry to be anywhere but be exactly where you were, only the roar of the daily bread van into the village reminded me I was in the twentieth century. Who cared if the fly-spotted electric bulb tremored and died. I much preferred evenings when the hiss of the ammonia gas flared erratically and caste green, purplish light on the walls of the bar.

Every day crammed. Embedding ourselves in its culture We swam, explored the hillsides above the lake and mostly stayed close to Ruesga.

If we had the urge to explore further afield, we'd drive the twenty-five miles of twisty gravel around the reservoir to where the remote village of Triollo lay tucked below the distant mountain of Curavaca. We didn't go there often, but when we did our favorite thing was to hike Curavaca's river valley beyond the village and follow its a tumbling river to picnic on its banks and take a dip in a deep swimming hole we'd discovered. Back at the car, we made a point of stopping at Triollo's small cantina to devour slices of local cheese and *jamon* before heading back to Ruesga.

A school friend of mine had been thrown out of Spain where she had a job as a holiday tour guide. Her crime: being a single woman and throwing wild parties with no chaperon present. Knowing the concept of Common-law Marriage would never be tolerated in Generalissimo's Catholic Spain, Ed and I allowed people to assume were legally wed, for in our eyes and the law of England that's what we were. Married. Husband. Wife.

And I'm glad we did or our eleven summers in Ruesga couldn't have happened. Most likely we'd been ostracized for sure, labeled as amoral, and certainly never, never been welcomed in the village the way we were.

For the first time in Ed's and my relationship we functioned as a family. That the boys never called Ed papa, I guess people thought natural to those weird foreigners.

Too shy to go off on their own, and uncomfortable as we were of being stared at, for the first couple of days, Anthony and Miles stayed glued to my side. At odd moments we'd catch sight of Mercedes' youngest son, Javi. Peeping round a corner or from behind a door eyes wide gazing at us, the *estranjeros*, as if we had two heads. His curiosity finally won. Javi came and stood boldly in front us and inspected the boys.

"Holá. Antonio y Milo," we introduced the boys using the Spanish adaptation of their names his mother used.

Next moment the three of them were gesturing and giggling together as if they understood each other's every word. That was it. They were off 'adventuring' for the rest of the day just as I hoped. Hours later, like Pied Piper, Javi lead them back to us usually followed by a gang of village children. Sunburned, with their hair on end, clothes rumpled and legs scratched and dirty, garbling tales of chasing hens, catching snakes and hay fights Anthony and Miles called their see you tomorrows.

On our way to collect water from the spring one early evening that first week, a pitching tidal wave of black and brown long-eared goats funneled between the buildings of Ruesga's narrow street completely surrounding us. Barely taller than the animals, for a moment I feared Anthony and Miles might be scared, or even be swept along by the spate.

Then as quickly as they'd appeared, the flock passed. All woolly backs, flapping ears and wriggling stumpy tails, small groups broke off in twos and threes splintering into smaller and smaller groups along the street as each arrived at the arched doorway of their own home.

Locked out, bleating to be let in and be fed and milked, they littered the street with nervous droppings as each goat strained to catch their owner's welcoming whistle.

Eyes darting, self-conscious as any human caught out in a foolish mistake, one or two lone members of the group, jerked their heads checking this way and that, then realized they waited outside the wrong door. Twitching long ears, the interlopers suddenly extricated themselves and scurried back to conceal themselves in the flock. Then poof, courtyard doors swung open and every goat was gone.

"Oh, those goats," we laughed. "They looked so human."

The boys of course had the advantage over us. Every Ruesgan, both men and women loved and tolerated every child they met children and before the end of week one, called out to them by name. I could see Ed felt a little envious for acceptance was something he desperately wanted.

4

EASING IN

"Look at that guy," Ed whispered our very first evening in Ruesga indicating the younger of three men propped in the dark corner of the Juanon Bar studiously ignoring us. "Shoulders on him like an ox. Totally hypnotic."

Five feet of brawn, a man in his forties, his voice dominated the conversation. I caught his eye for a second and felt myself falling into an abandoned well beyond the reach of daylight.

"What a face. Should they ever accept us, I'd love to take his photograph. He'd make a great portrait." I agreed, trying not to stare.

The man stood out from his companions. Something about the baby innocence of his face, the way he smiled pushing back the *boina* on his head to expose a moonlike dome of white from beneath his beret, and a gap where once a tooth had rooted. Mahogany brown, broad-chested, not an ounce of fat on his body, the three buttons of the man's checked shirt lazed open at the neck revealing a non-too-clean a triangle of under-vest which he'd stuffed roughly into a pair of baggy work trousers. Nobody it seemed wore boots. Like every-one we'd seen so far, he wore a pair of blue canvas espadrilles trodden flat at the heel.

"Anyway, till the locals get used to me, I've decided to hang out in the bar for a couple of hours each evening and break the barrier. I really want to make friends. You staying?" Ed asked.

"No way. Not me. I'm off outside to sit with the boys."

Without Spanish, I found the atmosphere far too intimidating. Even if I stuck close to Ed. The stares. The sudden silence made me feel a trespasser. A woman, I mostly stayed well away, but with no place to hang out apart from our room upstairs or on the wall outside, I was forced to occasionally invade the male domain. When I did, I felt as conspicuous as if I were naked.

"See you later," Ed ordered another *vino* and leaned forward leaning one elbow on the bar.

Luckily daylight didn't fade till well after nine at that latitude, so we had no problem staying outside till cena appeared on the table and Ed joined us in Mercedes' kitchen

For the following evenings, determined to make contact with the locals however long it took, Ed ensconced himself at the far end of the bar straining to capture the odd word from the thunderclaps of Castilian reverberating about him.

"Hear that? They never stop. Nobody just speaks. They all bellow. You've never heard such a din," he related when he finally snuggled into bed beside me.

Men's voices and occasional guffaws of laughter penetrated the floorboards into our room. *Coño. Cabrón.* Swear words boomed loud and clear. A bang of the front door, and then sudden silence.

Pointedly ignored by the locals, three days Ed drank alone staring at his glass. The three men's backs, a clear signal they wanted him, *estranjero*, gone. Not Ed. He saw their rejection as a challenge to stay put.

But on the fourth day, finally, finally, after perhaps, a few too many *claretes*, the younger man of the three who according to Ed, seemed to virtually live in the Juanon, with a flip of his head tossed a wordless *Buenas* in his direction without a break in whatever he was talking about to his friends.

"I exist," he crowed excitedly to me later when he returned to our room. "Ox-Shoulders actually nodded to me."

The next evening it happened. The same man who'd nodded buenas the previous evening addressed him. Face to face. Verbally.

"Alejandro." Expressionless, the man fixed his eyes on Ed and pointed to himself.

"Alejandro? *Soy Ed. Mucho gusto.*" He tentatively repeated back with his newly mastered Berlitz phrase.

"*Una ronda,*" Ed signaled Juan to fill his and the glasses of those present. Ed shook his head describing the interchange. "Anyway, my round of *clarete* seemed to break the ice."

Alejandro pulled a crumpled packet from his pocket and surprised Ed by selecting and handing him a single fag with his forefinger and thumb. At the same time the bar owner, Juan leaned over offering him a light from a curious looking metal tube through which dangled a knotted yellow cord. Striking the flint repeatedly, he cupped his hands around the spark he'd made gently blowing till its end glowed orange. *Cigarete* dangling, curious, Ed turned the strange object over and over in his hands before returning it.

"*Metcha,*" Juan held the object up naming it.

"*Metcha,*" Ed repeated and scribbled the new word in the small notebook he kept in his shirt pocket.

"I'm sure I've seen something similar in a museum somewhere," he described the exchange excitedly when I joined him later at the bar before *Cena.* "In the second World War, POWs made these in the camps from the thick inside seams of their pajama legs. Soaked in saltpeter they work as well as any match. I'm going to look for one in Cervera when we next go to town," he announced.

Ed tapped his chest and pointed to me. "Ed. Isabel," he encouraged turning to his new friends.

I don't know why he called me Isabel, or how it came to be Isabel became my Spanish name.

"Si. Isabel," I liked the ring of *Isabel.* I even used it myself.

"Alejandro. Juanillio. Leandro," each man named himself.

Juanillio, the older man with a toothless smile lifted his glass.

"Vaso," cupping his hand, he emphasized each syllable.

"Vaso," Ed repeated.

"Vaso, glass " I reiterated.

"Vino," Juanillio plunged his thumb towards his clenched fist pouring imaginary wine.

"Beber," he annunciated carefully pointing his thumb towards his open mouth. Spreading his fingers, he tilted back his head and mimed himself gulping.

"Glass. Wine. Drink." We laughingly translated, imitating his actions.

From those three most important words of Spanish, our vocabulary grew, and I came to realize if I stayed quietly in my place, I, a woman and a foreigner would be accepted too.

"Nuestros Professores de Espanol", Ed jokingly dubbed our teachers *Professore de Cultura.* Pondering his title, Alejandro paused rubbing his fingers under the rim of his *boina.* Then he smiled.

"Si, professore, sujo," he repeated and nodded proudly. From then on, Alejandro became our self-appointed guide.

That, my first impression, is how I picture Alejandro, the man who became our friend, the man through whose eyes we learned to see another way to live, and to read a little of the language ploughed into the land.

Though others in the village teased Alejandro calling him a simpleton and saying it was only his *boina* that kept the moonlight from scrambling the contents of his head, he laughed with them liking their teasing, their attention. Being included.

Evenings, midday, the Juanon Bar became our class room. After a full day of exploring, swimming, hiking in the mountains, the bar was the perfect place to cool off. Being a Language Professor Ed could quickly detect the regional differences in how the people spoke.

"La(s) mora(s) ma(s) rica(s)," Ed sing-songed dropping the final S on words and holding his nose in imitation of the Southern Spanish

nasal twang. Alejandro couldn't stop laughing. I still remember the phrase. The sound of the word *mora(s)* for blackberries.

Ed, his willing pupil, Alejandro took his Professor-role seriously. Well not too seriously, their exchanges became childishly silly, ridiculous even as the two of them deepened their friendship. With exaggerated lip movements, Alejandro annunciated a new, and too often vulgar word for Ed to repeat, and then collapse laughing at his attempt.

Boring the second time, I played ignorant pretending I didn't understand.

Ed took out his notebook. Held his pencil ready.

"Hijo de puta...jodere...maricon...me cargo in la leche..." Ed's vocabulary of profane, swearwords grew.

"Salut y pesetas, health and money,*"* joining them, Leandro raised his glass in a toast. *"...y una motha con buenas tetas.* and a girl with beautiful tits.*"*

"Sangre de Christo.... Blood of Christ," and raising a glass of red, kissed the base of the glass in mock benediction of the Priests at Holy Communion," they blasphemed. "But shh, don't let the Guardia hear, or it's off to the *cárcel."* He crossed his wrists as though in handcuffs.

Early on the first week after Ed stood his friends several rounds, it came time to pay up.

Holding a handful of coins in his open palm, *peseta,* by *peseta,* Ed counted out each coin onto the bar.

"Mas tarde." Flat faced, Juan the owner shook his head brusquely. He ignored the coins.

Nonplussed, Ed and I glanced at each other. It was days later before we understood. By counting out each coin to settle the tab, it turned out Ed unknowingly committed a cultural blooper. He'd insulted Juan. Implied Ed didn't trust him.

"It's what those *cabrónes, los Allemanes,* the German hikers, did when they stopped by for a *vino* a few months back. You should have seen the buggers. Checking and re-checking the small change Juan gave them, anyone would think they'd been cheated of a million *pesetas."* Alejandro sniffed dismissing the entire German population.

"Animales, you mean" Juanillio, his toothless friend, laughingly corrected, relishing the play on words.

Caught up in their remembering, Alejandro and Juanillio wouldn't let the subject drop. We watched Alejandro imitate the German tourist. Staring at the imaginary coin change lying on his palm. Counting, recounting each *peseta* as if some were missing.

The innocent foreigner was likely only puzzling over the unfamiliar currency just as Ed and I had those first days in Spain. No point in explaining, though, their minds were made up.

"Estranjeros. Cochones," he spat the insult. Foreigners. Pigs.

"Oh. But not you. You're not like them," Alejandro corrected quickly with a sidelong glance at Ed. "You're different. You're from over the water. You're alright."

Juanillio, nodded vigorously in agreement. Smiled reassuringly showing his pink gums.

Alejandro threw his arm over Ed's shoulder and pulled him close to his side without removing his arm. Un-used to physical contact between men, I saw Ed flinch as if he'd been assaulted.

Ed never counted change again in Spain. He trained himself to casually throw a handful of *pesetas* on the bar and look away while Juan helped himself to what was owed.

"You can leave any extra change as a token thank-you," Alejandro added. "That's not insulting. But stop saying thank-you. You do it all the time."

Our appointed *Professor de Cultura*, Alejandro instructed seriously.

"Porque?" Ed questioned.

Alejandro shrugged, but had no answer.

"Who ever heard of such a thing," Ed and I exchanged glances and dismissed what he told us.

Mercedes nodded when I checked with her later.

"He's right. Saying thank-you, obligates the recipient to return the favor."

"Hmm." I couldn't argue with her logic. Put like that perhaps it made total sense.

Later, as we sat down to *Comida*, I asked Mercedes if we should or should not say *gracias* when someone gave us something…a glass of wine, a gift, a kindness.

"*Gracias y por favor* are reserved for priests," she sniffed disparagingly, though I never understood the logic.

But a lifetime habit of polite pleases and thank-yous were hard for me to unlearn, and when she returned and placed our meal on the table, an instinctive gracias slipped from between my lips.

"What are you a priest now?" Mercedes mocked making a face.

It took all summer to train ourselves and bite our tongues to prevent an unguarded gracias from escaping. Soon the new habit came naturally. No need to voice gratitude, a smile was thanks enough. Give. Accept. Like our village friends taught me, the acts of giving and receiving were simply those. No expectation. Uncomplicated. Simple. We knew we'd graduated when Juan handed Ed a single fag in his fingers, and Ed took it, placed it between his lips with a nod, leaned forward to light it from Juan's *metcha* without a thank-you.

Though Alejandro never introduced or invited us to his home or to meet his family that first year, Ed's and Alejandro's faces lit up whenever they met. A tall, well-read literary professor who worked in a university's academic clouds, and a man half his height unable to either write or read a word of script yet could interpret the indecipherable (to Ed) language of the earth and sky, made for a strange mix of mutual respect. Their genuine pleasure at being in the other's company was strangely charming to watch. A perfect balance of give and take I decided.

Since childhood I'd loved the beauty of botanical and local names of wild plants. Campion. Stork's Bill. Shepherd's purse. Jack-in-the-pulpit.

"What's the name for this, Alejandro?" I asked holding up a wildflower for him to see wanting to add its Spanish name to my vocabulary.

"*Una flor,*" a flower, he looked at me strangely.

She doesn't even know what a flower is. The woman must be daft, I read his mind.

Same thing with tools, machines, and the many other familiar objects I wanted identified. Threshing, harrowing, winnowing, a machine was a machine, a tree a tree, and a flower a flower. Hopeless. I gave up.

"Una machina," he'd explain carefully. No specific label necessary, its use was perfectly clear to Alejandro.

We became sunflower seed addicts, and munched them between sips of wine. One *peseta* bought you a packet. But with no saucer, ashtray in sight, what to do with the *pipas* husks cupped in our palms shells we wondered?

Alejandro put a sunflower seed between his front teeth, and parrot-like then separated the nut with his tongue and spat out the husk.

"Chuck them on the floor," he indicated pointing to the litter. "Crack the seeds like this."

Shocked, I watched him casually spit a couple across the room to join the mounting pile of tossed *cajacuete* and *pipas* husks, olive pips, shrimp tails, mussel shells and potato crisp bags on the floor.

It took an act of will to obey the first time, but with no choice of where else to dispose of our pipas shells, forced myself to follow suit and let the accumulating stash in my hand slip surreptitiously to the floor. Giggling together like naughty children I remember how wicked the four of us felt throwing trash on the floor.

"Shall we really, Mum?" Anthony and Miles asked surprised staring at the mess.

Though there were no tea leaves to scatter and tamp down the mess as in the Elizabethan era, Mercedes and her daughter, Upe, swept the debris out through the door and into the dust every hour or so and leave the floor clean.

Throwing our trash to the floor became so ingrained a habit, one time, Ed and I were newly back at the Jolly Gardeners pub in proper-old-England, I casually hurled a crisp bag and a handful of peanut shells at the barman's feet. I've never seen a man jump so high. Ducking to escape the attack, he leaped backward as if I'd hurled a cricket ball at his chest.

"Oh sorry. So Sorry," I collapsed laughing. "I forgot this isn't Spain."

5

FIRST FIESTA

The jangled crash of the church bell bounced off our bedroom wall rattling the open window.

"What's going on?" Jerking myself awake, I elbowed Ed's back.

"Kids...fiesta," he mumbled sleepily rolling onto his side.

"But at four am? Really?"

Little point pulling the sheet and pillow over my head. Staggering to the window I peered into the dark. Nothing. Not one light glimmered, only the stars. Then as suddenly, the cacophony silenced.

I clomped back to the warm hollow in the wool mattress I'd just abandoned and wriggled the stuffing to fit my body shape. A couple of deep breaths and I vanished into the beyond of the dreamworld

I'd hardly closed my eyes it seemed, when sunbeams fingered their way through the shutters tickling my face. I lay a moment allowing the thunk of cowbells from the lane below, and the clacks of storks' beaks from the church tower to filter the room, but when a chorus of roosters added to the carousing, I knew it was time to get up.

I looked over at Ed. Still snoring, faint puffs parted his lips. I slid out of bed, pulled on my clothes, and tip-toed from the room.

"Morning, my darlings," I called, pushing open the boys' bedroom door. Sheets tucked in, pillows in place, both Anthony's and Miles' beds were empty.

I found them both outside perched quietly on the wall sitting in the lengthening patch of morning sunshine. Ties, clean shirts and shorts, their hair slicked into place they looked so cute in their fiesta outfits.

"There you are. My, don't you both look sharp." I bent and kissed each cheek before settling beside them. "Ed should be down soon."

I loved these gentle beginnings of each day, our early wait for breakfast watching the village slowly come to life before the sun exploded. No telephone pole, no electric wire to carve the view with ugly lines, no sound of motor to disturb the calm as goats, cows and people spilled from *quadro* doors.

Though we'd been in Ruesga no more than a couple of weeks, I was beginning to feel less and less like an outsider and more and more part of a familiar pattern.

Buen dia. Same each morning, a woman I recognized only by the mattock she carried over one shoulder, and the empty basket in her hand, nodded shyly as she headed down the lane towards the meadow and acknowledged our presence.

"Buen dia, senora," I called and add in English "There she goes, boys. Off to dig her vegetables. Let's see what she'll choose today."

When I sat on the wall alone with no Ed, no children beside me, when a man walked by it was different. Unchaperoned I clearly didn't exist. Eyes fixed straight ahead, even Alejandro, Ed's new friend from the bar, sidled past no more than a dozen feet away behind his herd of six cows without a glance in my or the boys' direction.

"Hup. Hup", he'd urge his cows spotting us.

Dropping his head, he stared studiously at the ground as the

cows plodded by to drink at the river. And then again as they returned with dripping chins to the safety of their *quadro* leaving wet
tracks on the dirt behind them.

"Good timing, Ed," I greeted as he stepped into the sunlight.
"My stomach's grumbling."

Mercedes must have been listening out for him, for at the same
moment Ed emerged outside to join us, her cheery voice called us
from the doorway.

"Desayuno." Mercedes announced. *"Buenas Dias. Desayuno,"*

A sunflower, light falling on her greying hair, she greeted us from
the open doorway and I couldn't help but catch her smile. No mourner's black for her. No headscarf clamped over her curls, tiny blue
and pink flowers patterned the apron she tied covering her dress. A
dependable, no-nonsense woman, convention was not for her. She
forged a path not typical for a village woman. Ran a bar. Rented out
rooms. Served meals to strangers. I felt warm in her presence. As if
I belonged.

Mercedes ushered us indoors fussing around the boys, fingering
the boys' neatly knotted ties.

"Fiestas hoy. Que guapos eres," she complimented.

Shivering in the kitchen's sudden coolness, I wrapped my hands
around the steaming bowl of milk Mercedes set at my place wishing
it were coffee. Real coffee, not the powdered Nescafe or cocoa the
Spanish seemed to enjoy to start their day. I reached for one of the
dry Marie biscuits and a sponge Madelaine cupcake already set out
on a plate.

We blew onto our scalding drinks, sipped, and dipped our dry
biscuits to a soggy mass in the most un-English way in our hurry to
be done with our meal and escape back outside.

"Saved by the bell," Ed smiled pushing back from the table as a
peal of bells crashed deafeningly from the church tower.

"Now to see what a Spanish Fiesta is all about."

In the short time we'd been inside eating breakfast, about thirty
people now milled outside on the wider section of road in the front
of the church. I didn't recognize half the faces and supposed friends
and family traveled from the town of Cervera, and the scattering

of hamlets around the lake. I felt a little awkward, an outsider not taking part, and stepped backwards flattening myself into the shadows watching, staring, as the black clothed crowd jostled into two orderly lines.

Pulling a last drag on their smokes then heeling their still glowing butts into the dirt three musicians emerged from the shade and sauntered to the head of the procession. Straightening their ties and tucking in their shirts, each man picked up his instrument, a trumpet, drum, and accordion, and blasted a mournful chord over the heads of the somber crowd.

Ed and I exchanged glances. I'd somehow expected laughter and shouts of *Olé, Olé,* all the cliched images of fiestas I associated with flamboyant southern Spain: spinning wheels of bright flamenco skirts and glossy red lip-sticked women with alluring carnations behind their ears.

"Not exactly jolly," I whispered rolling my eyes. "All that black."

Just as the notes of the cord died, the drum rolled, the church doors creaked open and the Virgin Mary appeared, an arum lily in her hand. A vision. The gold trims and paisley swirls patterning her dress, blinding in the sun light forced me to lower my gaze. Delicate, pale, palm stretched forward, smiling, she offered us her saintly blessing. Gazing at the crowd from her platform her body seemed to float as she was carried by. Not me for I didn't know the form, but as one the crowd bobbed their knees and made the sign of the cross. I saw one old woman fall to the ground and put her lips to the earth.

Though I'm neither Catholic nor particularly religious, I swear I felt a wave of peace emanating from the Virgin as her statue passed. Serene, angelic, her blue eyes fixed on the unseen, swaying unsteadily in the sunlight, she paused at the head of the procession.

Anthony and Miles in front, me behind, my hands light on their shoulders, we stood together a little apart from the crowd. Ceremony always catches me unawares, embarrasses me with a sudden tug of emotion at my gut. Fearful I might weep, I pressed them to me and kissed the top of each head.

I looked around. No sign of Alejandro, his brother, sister, nor any of the Juanon family. We had no idea then, how much they, and half the village it turned out, would have nothing to do with the Catholic church.

"Look Mum. Over there. That's Ed's friend, the man with one eye." Anthony and Miles tugged me towards a balding man in the middle of the line frantically signaling for us to join him.

"Can we? Can we?"

"Leandro? Is that you? *Es possible por nuestros...?*" My Spanish petering, I reverted to sign.

Scrubbed, clean-shaven and without his *boina* and work clothes I scrutinized him to make sure the smartly dressed man really was Ed's pal.

"Hey, Ed," I beckoned. "Come join us. Leandro says we can walk with him."

"No way. Not my thing." Making a face Ed shook his head. "I'll be at the bar."

And he headed for the Juanon with a wave, pausing a moment to watch the procession set off on its slow-march through the village.

Caught up in the mood of the occasion, Anthony and Miles moved to either side of Leandro, clasped their hands piously and bowed their heads. A little self-consciously, I did the same and became a penitent on a sacred pilgrimage seeking God and my soul. Caught off guard by a sudden emotion, I wiped away a shameful tear. Processional music always does that to me.

The sun wiped every shadow from our path so by the time the procession reached the upper end of the village I had broken into a sweat. No escape. Each slow step became a mile. At the rate we were going I felt we'd never get back to the church. The tolling of a single bell calling the villagers to Mass thankfully silenced the dismal dirge as we approached the church.

The boys and I hung back allowing the crush of people to stream inside before sliding into the very last pew. Cool at last, I looked around surprised to see almost every pew taken. I'd no idea so many Catholics lived in this tiny village as I thought from the reaction of our friends at least half the population wouldn't set foot in the place.

Waiting for the service to begin, I took time to take in my surroundings; the triangle of sunlight invading the cold stone aisle from the open door behind us where we sat; the startling carpet of red and yellow sprays of gladioli strewn below the white altar cloth; the expectant silence blanketing the air as the congregation settled and shifted positions.

I stared aghast the same old woman I'd noticed outside earlier, struggle past our pew walking on her stockinged knees led by a young girl. The old woman's agony. The pleading in her eyes. Her atonement of imagined sins. I shook my head repulsed, sat back into the silence and contemplated her painful sacrifice. Five, ten minutes ticked by. I tapped my watch-less wrist.

On the stroke of twelve, the massive church doors clanged shut trapping us into a dimly lit world heavy with the scent of decaying flower petals and musty stone. The purple and gold-robed priest materialized from a cloud of incense flanked by his trio of white-robed altar boys, two bearing candles and a third leading with a cross.

"Thank goodness, about time," I muttered to myself rising to my feet with the silent crowd. Clearly loving the drama, Anthony stood when the congregation rose, sat, genuflected and crossed himself copying what he saw. Thankful to be at the back, I rolled my eyes at Miles and set him giggling. The only part of the Service I found moving were the intoned chants and hymns sung Catholic style.

In call and response, full-throated, in Spanish, they sang of glory, of salvation and gave thanks. Unable to join in I closed my eyes and flew on the tidal swell of male and female voices to the rafters.

Scanning his flock as if looking for vermin, I took an instant dislike to the priest the moment he began his preaching.

Straining to catch the priest's bellowed diatribe, it took me a moment to hear he was speaking in Spanish and not Latin.

"*Señor. El.* He,*"* the priest jabbed a thumb over his shoulder indicating Jesus. "*Yo.* I," he thumped his chest, "and *ustedes*, you," he sneered glaring at us, his captive audience.

I couldn't believe what I was hearing.

Bang, before I could make a move to get out of there, the priest crashed his fist onto the lectern.

"And now…" he paused, "the scriptural teaching of the day."

"Enough. Come Miles," I signaled and tapping Anthony's shoulder, the three of us made for the door.

6

AN ALL DAY AFFAIR

"I just had to get out of there." I exploded to Ed. "I thought that supercilious priest was about to damn the lot of us to hell." I almost bit the small glass Ed handed me.

Ed pushed back from the stone bar making room for me to squeeze in beside him, Alejandro and Leandro.

"It's a madhouse," I screeched reaching for a stuffed olive. "Buen fiesta. Wow, what a crush." I shouted again aware I couldn't be heard.

I looked hungrily at the line of *tapas* stretched the length of the stone bar. *Langostinos, sardinas, manchego* cheese, chickpeas in garlic, *jamon*, yumm. What to choose?

I picked out a Sunday-only treat, *Tor-e-as*. A neatly halved hard-boiled egg smeared with mayonnaise, on which teetered a tower of sliced onion, green chili, sweet red pimento topped by half an anchovy green and an olive. Speared tenuously together by a toothpick, the only possible way to eat it without making a mess was to pop the whole thing in at once.

"Here goes." With a quick look around to see if anyone was watching, opening my mouth wide I pouched in the whole creation feeling a little like a hamster, and covered my over-stuffed cheeks with my hand. Shrimp tails and peanut shells rained onto the floor. The volume spiked as cheeks flushed red as the wine that flowed. Mine included, no doubt. I retreated from the waves of words battering my ears and smiled as if I were listening.

All heads swiveled towards the church crowd outside as a tirade of pops and bangs and the smell of acrid smoke and laughter assailed the Juanon.

"Fiesta's really beginning. Let's go," and picking up our glasses we headed for the door.

"Mum, look what Javi gave us." Anthony and Miles held up a strip of a paper then laughing, hurled it to the ground. Bang. I jumped behind Ed's back. But there was no escape, firecrackers exploded all around me as they and every village kid set on scaring us adults run for their lives. Harmless fun, I laughed along.

Snatches of accordion, violin and drum music pierced the noise. I turned to locate the source. Arraigned along the shade-line of the church wall, almost unrecognizable in blue and red short sleeved shirts, and jackets gone, those same three musicians from the morning's procession tapped happy feet in dance, and burst into the occasional celebratory *Olé*. The drummer, all the while, dragging life blood from a ciggy he kept dangling from the corner of his mouth.

The crowd swung suddenly apart to make room for a group of teenagers trying to manhandle the strangest wooden saddle-shaped contraction onto the back of one of their companions.

Instantly surrounded by a forest of thrusting hands clamoring me-me, the boys fought to grab a proffered firework and stick theirs into one of the empty holes till the whole saddle-holder was stuck all over with fireworks like porcupine quills.

Once filled it took three strong men to jostle the firework-laden contraption into place on their friend's broad shoulders.

"Burn them. Burn them."

Louder and louder, the crowd's chant insisted, then suddenly hushed. I watched the young men step forward holding aloft a flaming torch.

"Quema. Quema-lo," the cry increased as the oldest boy prepared to torch the wick of every firework strapped to his friend's back.

"Atras. Atras," his young friends shouted shooing back the watching crowd to a marginally safer distance.

"Olé. Olé," the crowd goaded

It took me a moment to understand what was brewing. The young man, bent double, lowered his head shook his head like an enraged bull and charged.

"They can't be serious," I gasped watching a Roman candle skim the heads of bystanders. Whoosh. A rocket soared over the church, a succession of others over the roofs. Whoosh, one exploded into the row of chopos, poplar trees, by the bridge. Twisting his body this way and that, the bull appeared to deliberately aim the exploding fireworks at the scattering crowd. The more the danger, the more the spectators laughed and squealed.

"This is madness. Someone could be seriously hurt," I screamed at Ed in disbelief as a shower of incandescent colored sparks rained on the crowd.

But he couldn't hear me over the bangs, and whistles.

Hands pressed to my ears, wildly pushing through the crowd, I located Anthony and Miles and ignoring their outrage, dragged them from their Spanish friends to the safety of the Juanon.

"Inside. Now. You can watch from inside the bar." I screamed pushing them through the doorway till every rocket and squib spent the show was over. No-one had been burned. Nobody hurt. Anthony and Miles bolted from the bar to join their friends to grab the spent cardboard carcasses littering the ground.

Pumped revelers funneled past me back into the Juanon shouting and laughing so loudly I felt I'd been dropped into a madhouse. *Clarete*, blanco, tinto, excited calls fired all around me. To survive it was Join in or die, I decided. So join in I did.

"Feliz fiestas," I yelled at everybody and no-one in particular as

I wormed my way through the heave of waving arms to reach and Ed and Alejandro. I found his brother, Ignacio and brother-in-law, Mariano had joined them. I'd not met Mariano before and he said not a word as we were introduced. Half smiling, his fingers timidly brushed mine, childlike, he surveyed me with watery blue eyes for the fraction of the second we connected.

"Mucho gusto," Ignacio thrust out his hand his eyes boldly stripping me of my dress, his left palm squeezing a little too intimately to mine as he did so. It was then I noticed his right hand. Withered, his fingers curled unevenly about his glass.

"Creepy letch," I spat in English under my breath giving him the cold eye. Pulling back, I moved closer to Ed's side.

"Clarete for my friends," unaware of what had just passed, Ed waved to attract Upe's attention.

Syllables I made no sense of imploded in my head. The only way to survive, I decided was to draw an invisible curtain across the noise and focus on the people and their interactions in the crowded bar. I felt invaded by the crush. Not them. Elbows touching, pink-faced from the heat and a little too much celebrating, the men carried on seemingly unconcerned by the squeeze, shamelessly spitting and dropping shrimp heads, tails, pipas shells and olive pits on the floor. How did they manage to keep up drinking all that wine? *Desayuno, Comida* midday, *Merienda* late afternoon, evenings in the bar, and again more *clarete* at home with their *cena.* Yet I only ever saw one man unable to hold his drink: *El Boracho,* the drunk, people called him, a sad and lonely alcoholic I'd seen in a Cervera bar.

Turning my attention back to our group, I looked at Ed, the way he rattled on jabbering away like a local, one arm flung casually over Alejandro's shoulder. German, French, and now Spanish it seemed, came so easily to him, while there I was, poor me, still fumbling along in pigeon Spanish. Who'd guess a month back he spoke no more than half a dozen words. I sighed envyng him his gift for languages.

Looking around the bar, I became aware of the number of women there with their husbands. Usually I was the only one. Special allowance for fiesta, I decided. Not fidgeting, still as statues, looking as if they could stand all day, I watched them sip their cokes and some garish orange liquid through paper straws. Surprised at seeing me as I was them, we briefly glanced at one another careful not to catch the other's eye. What's she doing here drinking with a bunch of men, I guessed their disapproval, or was it envy at the freedom of my un-covered head and arms, my unstockinged legs?

My feet ached. Two hours at least of standing on unforgiving stone, and not a chair in sight. Enough. Desperate to get off my poor feet, and needing to sit and eat soon or collapse I was about to head off outside when Anthony and Miles ran up saying lunch was ready. And like an angel, Mercedes signaled from the doorway with-out putting a toe into the bar. Though she had been at it, chopping, slicing and cooking up small plates of tapas since early morning, barely a hair was out of place.

"*Ahora. Comida,*" she beckoned calmly as if Fiesta was a regular day,

I wanted to fling my arms around her.

Lunch over, she shooed us upstairs. "*Ahora siesta. Baille tarde,*" she instructed.

Siesta? Easier said than done. Booming voices from below, and amplified screeches and thrumps from mis-tuned mics battered the glass panes even through the closed window.

"*Si. Si. Non. Non,*" reverberated through the village over the next couple of hours.

"How ever many times do they need to si-si-non test those damn things," I exclaimed shaking my head

"That's it. I give up." Ed swung his legs to the floor and stood up.

After tossing and turning for more than an hour, we admitted defeat and dragged ourselves downstairs to join the children on *la Era* for the fiesta's final celebration.

Outside, the fading light intensified every sensation. The heat from the buildings and arched-doored *quadros*, the very beaten earth of the lane, whiffs and sounds of country odors, grass, and dung, and meadow flowers bombarded me as I passed. I squeezed Ed's arm feeling an inexplicable surge of joy.

"Happy?" I asked.

No mistaking where the *Baille* was being held. The music made sure of that. Arm in arm Ed and I followed its loud beat to Maria's Bar at the upper end of the village, and from there up the short slope opposite onto the threshing field they called *la Era*.

Lit up like a party cruise ship adrift in a limitless ocean, the squared off dance floor in the one small corner of the threshing field heaved with crazed giant shadows of wildly flinging arms and legs across the uneven grass.

I don't know quite how I expected a fiesta dance would be, but the garish transformation, the gaudy display of fake frivolity violated its emptiness, the memory I held. The calm bustle of working men, of plodding cows, the hiss of sledges, the golden circles of grain.

A few adults jiggled stiffly beside their children. The same three musicians from earlier, collars loosened, hammered up-beat dance tunes into their mics from a rickety wooden platform that had mushroomed overnight. Disappointed I took in the gloomy affair trying to think back to the last time I'd danced.

Could it have been before Miles was born? Before my divorce. Before I moved back to England. I sighed overcome by a sense of loss I couldn't quite place. Perhaps the security of a forever marriage. The legal kind. The kind with a ring. The kindly face of the children's father came to me in my mind. The heartbreak in his eyes I caused when I left.

"Let's wait a bit for things to warm up," I said expunging the thought.

Not yet dark enough for partnering up, shadowy figures gathered around the white square of light. Their young lives still full of hope. Girls in one cluster, boys in another. Watching. Separate. Too shy to bridge the gap.

A few brave girls emerged slowly from the dark. Danced shyly with each other pretending to be unaware of the boys watching in the shadows waiting for their chance to pounce, to daringly hold hands, to lead a girl onto the dance floor and take her in their arms. Their mix of longing and anticipation the wanting and not wanting I smiled remembering my own tormented teenage years.

As if loosened from the earth, the moon's orb peeked low on the horizon, her curve resting on the reservoir's *presa* wall as if watching the antics below. My first sighting of a Harvest Moon I stared into the largest face I'd ever seen.

The tempo of the music geared into full swing. The dance floor filled. Arms in the air, couples flung themselves into *jota* after *jota*— the Spanish version of a Scottish Highland fling. I hung back studying the unfamiliar footwork of the dancers. *De da-de-da-di-da*. We couldn't resist its compelling rhythm.

"Come on. Even we can manage that." Ed took my hand and led me into the circle of light to leap and spin till we collapsed.

One-two-three hop, and a one-two-three… A lively polka started up, but we were out of puff.

"Too energetic for me. I'm ready for bed not that I'll ever sleep." I panted.

I was wrong. To the thumping beat of the music, I fell into an exhilarating dream-world of dance, where every leap catapulted me skyward before bouncing me back to earth, a handful of moonlight clutched in each palm.

Our summer ended ten days later. For the past evenings I'd noticed a dampness, a smell of summer dying, the smell of impending autumn.

Memories packed carefully in my bag, we shook hands with our new friends, hugged Mercedes and waved goodbye.

"*Hasta el anno qui viene*. Until next year," we called. Promised we'd be back.

"*Si. Si. Seguro*, for sure." Mercedes nodded politely.

Maybe all her guests told her the same for I could see her doubt.

Forlorn, the bramble and blackthorn in the hedgerows along the lane to Cervera already tinged with red and yellow drooped in the early morning light.

Yes, summer and we, were leaving Ruesga. I pulled my cardigan close around me.

7

TOY TOWN TENT

"Well, that's put the end of our two months at the Juanon in Ruesga," I screeched as the BBC newscaster announced the devaluation of our British pound. "Means the cost of the *peseta*'s now doubled."

Our plan to spend Anthony 's and Miles' summer school holidays in Spain exploded.

"We'll send each other mad cooped up in London for two-months." I clawed for a solution.

"How about camping?" Ed suggested. "I'm sure Mercedes would let us set up a tent in her meadow, particularly if we take occasional meals at the Juanon."

Clicking my ballpoint I listed what we'd need, most of which I had already moldering somewhere in either the attic or the house. Tents, blow-up beds. Sleeping bags. Kettle. Covered frying pan.

Washing up bowl… All but tents. Those we lacked. A large one for us, a small two-man for the boys.

"No worries mate. We know of a tent you can borrow," Ed's regular drinking pals, at the Jolly Gardeners Pub assented when he bemoaned our lack, and our proposed camping plan.

"I'll have you a 4-man tent here by tomorrow," his friend, Bernie winked, signaled Ed to ask no questions tapping his forefinger one side of his nose not elaborating. Odd. Ed thought, but not his problem.

That evening after dark, no doubt a little worse for wear, Bernie, his brothers, Terry and Norm, crept into a fellow boozer's garden, dismantled the orange tent shade house on the front lawn, and fled.

It was just a good lark. No harm in it, they reasoned, sniggering in anticipation of their friend's reaction when it reappeared it back on his lawn as mysteriously it had disappeared.

Ed thanked them with no idea the tent was stolen or that it was designed for play only. And of course, Bernie never said a word.

A week later, with the orange bundle strapped securely to the mini's roof rack, we waved the grey clouds goodbye and sailed for our second summer in sunny Spain.

Mercedes threw her arms about the boys exclaiming how they'd grown.

"You can put your tents in our meadow. Here," she escorted us down the short lane beside the Juanon. "And, the smaller tent for the boys there in the shade of that apple tree in the corner of the orchard.

Once we finally fixed poles, guy ropes and pegs in place and got the tent upright, never having camped in our lives, we thought the tent grand as a palace. Twelve-foot square, orange flap open, with three screened windows, we stood back proudly admiring the summer home we'd erected on the meadow grass.

The pink paisley cotton carpet I'd scored from a Charity Shop back home fitted perfectly inside the main tent. A folding table, four chairs, a blow-up mattress, suitcase for a bedside table, a box of utensils, a battery-powered lamp, our tent lacked nothing.

"Next, to make our kitchen, boys." Ed directed. "Who's coming with me to the river? We need three large smooth river stones."

A stone cradled to each chest, I watched them struggle back from the Pisuerga through the tall grasses.

"Look, what we found," panting, they dropped their burden beside the rectangular pit Ed hollowed in the grass.

Lined three sides with the stones, a grease-encrusted barbecue grill balanced across them and a pile of twigs, we had our kitchen.

"Now to christen it," I said striking a match and setting the kettle.

The four of us sat outside. Mugs of tea in our hands, the sun on our arms, no noise but our chatter and the call of songbirds, we looked at each other and grinned.

"Let's live like this for always," both boys agreed.

"Yes," I sighed. "This already feels like home."

No rain channel dug around the tents, no fly sheets, no built-in ground sheets, we might not have been so smug if Ed or I had known of such essentials.

"Alejandro," Ed exclaimed rising to his feet seeing him saunter through the gate. Arms around each other's shoulders, beaming like newly reunited brothers, off they went to the Juanon.

In between the boy's friends and villagers, I remembered from the previous year, dropping by to say welcome, the boys and I played house so we wouldn't have to scrabble searching around after dark. Bedding unrolled, pajamas under pillows, toothbrushes and paste in sight, we flashed SOS torch messages at one another before joining them a little later.

"Who's hungry? We're having supper with Mercedes."

Later, too enthralled by a sky of a billion stars that left no room for dark, eyes open, we lay snuggled into our sleeping bags. A shooting star, twinkling planet, fluttering bat, thudding moth, slivered moon lifting slowly from the trees, no way was sleep possible with such a show happening overhead.

"Look. Look. The North star...the Plough...Venus..." we called into the night till one by one, sleep silenced us.

I woke first. Crawled from our tent into a dew- soaked world.

How could we have been so stupid. Our carefully stacked wood lay soaked wet and useless beside a dismally soggy fire pit. I quashed the imaginary aroma of fresh brewed coffee, the smell and sizzle of frying bacon from my mind.

"Ed. Ed," I called. "That's it for hot water and breakfast."

However hard Ed blew and fanned the flaming twist of paper not one twig caught alight.

"It's the leftover packet of Marie biscuits and cold cereal this morning, I'm afraid kids," I moaned.

It didn't matter. A canteen of fresh milk begged from Mercedes, breakfast cereal eaten outdoors in the early light as the morning mist slowly evaporated from the meadow, we found ourselves in a magical world surrounded on three sides by mountains. And I knew then our summer would go well. And as if in agreement, the storks clacked their beaks from the church tower promising good luck.

I could already feel my skin burning. Our first day, and it would be a hot one.

"Just look at the blue sky. Isn't this glorious? Let's go for a swim." Ed suggested.

I followed him through the open tent flap and in less than a minute emerged covered with our clothes pulled modestly over our swimsuits.

"Ready, boys?" Swinging our towels, we headed through the village for the reservoir for our first swim of the year.

"The lake has shrunk since last year, but our diving rock has grown." Miles and Anthony chorused. It was true, the surface of the granite mass projected at least an extra meter from the water, and a wide band of dried mud and dead leaves ringed the shore's stony slope we claimed as our beach.

"Boy, they can't have had much rain, the water level is way down"

Not waiting to spread out our towels, we threw them in an untidy heap under the lone tree and raced to the water's edge.

"Don't splash. Don't splash," I called to the boys fending off a hail of drops.

Ankle deep, I paused a moment, a little shiver rippling down my spine. Delicious anticipation of cool, I took a breath and waded in, pushed far from shore. Drifting, leaf-like, motionless, gazing upward, the year's struggles melted into the pure vastness overhead.

We emerged reborn our hair slicked and dripping ready for the sun-filled days ahead.

Our only way to keep clean, we bathed in the lake nearly every day, drank wine each evening in the Lower Bar Juanon, and reconnected with Alejandro and the other regulars.

Off with their Spanish playmates, the boys disappeared to their favorite haunts for hours.

Our days blurred to a routine governed by the blazing sun. From mid-morning to late afternoon, we could have roasted a chicken inside both tents the heat generated by the canvas was so stiflingly hot. Not that we wanted to be inside anyway. Between snoring siestas and snack lunches in the shade of the apple orchard, swims at the lake, and hanging out at the Juanon, we kept cool enough.

My day began at the first light of day before Ed and the boys stirred when I lit and set our blackened kettle on the fire. Early morning tea, an English ritual I couldn't do without, gave me time to quietly wake. Empty of people at that hour, only birdsong filled the meadow.

All too soon sudden movements erupted from Anthony and Miles' tent as, jabbing and poking one another awake, each struggled to be first dressed and earn the right to fetch our canteen of still warm milk for breakfast from Mercedes.

"Buenas. Must have overslept. Coffee ready? What's for breakfast? I'm starving." Ed mumbled every morning, emerging from the tent unshaven.

Breakfasting around the fire after sun-up, before the heat of the day, snack lunch under the apple tree in, and a feast in the evening by the light of a hurricane lamp, no phone, no TV, no planes scribbling smoke trails in the sky, London's incessant bustle fell away.

Playing house, I called the chores required for tent-living, for they hardly seemed like work: stocking up on non-perishable supplies and fresh food, collecting firewood, I shopped in Cervera every couple of days. Bread came to the village by delivery van twice daily, drinking water from the village fountain, milk from Mercedes' cows, and wine from her bodega, we lacked for nothing. I became an expert at one-dish cuisine. Quail eggs, braised wild quail, chicken, rabbit and every variety of meat and vegetables, we dined by candlelight beneath the stars.

"I'd like to make a toast," I announced one evening over supper around the fire pit. "Here's to ten wonderful days under canvas. I think we've earned our gold star campers' badges. Here, Ed. Here, Anthony. Here, Miles. And one for me." I smiled handing a yellow dandelion flower to each and pushed a flower head through my shirt button.

"To us. To expert campers," we cheered raising our glasses.

Fatal words. Less than an hour later, the sun drew a veil across her orb.

"Looks like rain." I peered up at the overcast sky. "Better we eat early and turn in before dark."

I slipped inside my sleeping bag just as a fine drizzle filtered through the tent's flimsy cotton sprinkling my face. The sky cracked in two. A blast of thunder followed. Rain showered through the walls and from overhead.

"Wow. Now what?" Ed and I sat up at the same time, grabbed our plastic ponchos, towels, shopping bags, anything we could lay our hands on and covered our bedding. I snapped open my umbrella hoping to at least keep my face and pillow dry.

"Are you awake? Miles, Miles, how you doing over there? Are you both okay? Grab your ponchos and put up your umbrella. See if that works." I called into the dark. "But whatever you do, don't, don't touch the tent walls."

Too late of course, he and Anthony had already run their fingers along the wet canvas.

"Mum, the wet's coming in. We're getting soaked." I heard the panic in his voice.

"Us too. Let's see if we can stick it out for a little longer. It might stop," my voice wavered.

The canvas overhead began to sag. I had visions of us cramped together and shivering in the mini.

"Whatever the hell to do, Ed. We'll never make it through the night."

And as I spoke, the rainwater pooling on the roof broke through the thin cotton and crash-landed on the mattress.

"That's it. Quick, quick, boys, grab your raincoats and brollys. We'll have to make a run for it and wait the storm out in the bar."

"Everybody got your torches. Ready? One two three, go." Ed dove into the into the deluge grabbing Miles' hand as he ran.

Anthony and I followed. The beams of our flashlights almost useless, slipping and slithering, we had no choice but to splosh along the river of mud the lane had become to reach the Juanon.

The bar was shuttered, closed. Ed hammered on the door. Immediately the door flung open. Holding a flickering hurricane lamp, an angel, Mercedes stood in the doorway in a long nightshirt, a woolen shawl wrapped around her.

"Come in. Come in. I thought you'd be here sooner," she pulled us inside. "I have two beds ready, but you'll have to share a room."

As she spoke, Alejandro burst in behind us through the door water streaming from the black poncho slung over his shoulders.

"You can stay with me," he announced. "Ed can share my bed, the boys can sleep in with my brother, Ignacio, and you, Isabel can share my mother's bed."

I turned to Ed. "Ed, please explain that Mercedes has a room ready for us here."

"Muy aimable," I thanked, refusing the offer.

"God forbid," I muttered ungratefully under my breath, picturing La Madre's brass bed, its lumpy mattress, her unwashed legs caked with muck. And my boys lying close to Ignacio, a grown man obsessed with sex... That wouldn't be okay.

Water puddled on the floor. Anthony's and Miles' teeth chattered uncontrollably. Mercedes hustled Alejandro from the bar, locked up and held the lamp high.

"Upstairs with you," It was time to get dried off and into bed.

From the safety of our beds, dry and warm, tucked under blankets between crisp cotton sheets, we relived our ludicrous attempt to keep dry cocooned in ponchos, fight the bomb of water crashing through the cotton fabric with open umbrellas, and all the horrors of the night's disasters. At first loudly whispering, then louder and louder, each remembered detail seemingly funnier than the last, we exploded laughing hysterical with relief.

"Indoors. This is the only way to camp," we giggled. "We should write the Indoor Camper's guide. RULE ONE: PITCH TENT IN-SIDE A RAINPROOF BUILDING. RULE TWO: PITCH TENT CLOSE BAR. RULE THREE: KEEP UMBRELLAS HANDY IN CASE OF LEAKS: RULE FOUR.... Coming up with more and more ridiculous suggestions we laughed ourselves to sleep.

Next morning, though we'd not asked Mercedes to bother making breakfast, we stumbled sleepily downstairs to jugs of steaming milky coffee and chocolate waiting for us in her kitchen, along with a plate of our favorite sponge Madelaine cupcakes. We took our places round the table just as we used to the previous year when we lodged with her at the Juanon.

"Here we are back home with you, back with our Spanish family. Thank you, Mercedes for taking us in." Suddenly loving her, I reached for her.

She grabbed my outstretched hand and warmly squeezed.

"*Familia. Si. Nuestros.*" Her eyes softened. She smiled before quickly busying herself with something on the stove.

"Juan will dig you a channel all around the tent so you won't get flooded again. Next time there's a storm, don't wait so long. This is your home anytime you want," then added, "I expect you for lunch today. You'll have too much to sort out today to have time to cook."

Arms folded across her chest, she stood beside the table. A mother hen, watching, making sure we ate.

"Better check on last night's damage," Ed announced pushing back his chair.

Squelching single file behind him down the water-logged lane we made our way to the meadow. The sun belied the violence of the night's storm.

The air shimmered with that freshly washed smell that only rain can bring. Steam rose from every surface, the earth, the grass in the meadow, the apple tree's leaves, the fire pit and sagging tents.

Peeping apprehensively inside we found not one possession escaped the storm. Our bedding, the carpet I'd been so proud of, our clothes, and food-store lay crumpled and sodden. Nothing for it but to drag everything outside into the sun. Soon, the granite wall behind the tent, lower branches of the apple tree, every bush and patch of grass were covered beneath a crazy patchwork of our possessions. We were well into the clean-up by the time Juan strolled up. Without a word of criticism, he looked around, took in the situation, and nodded, then, swung his mattock and hacked the foot-wide rain channel we should have dug round the tent's perimeter if we'd been seasoned campers.

A camper's life is terrible 'ard says Alice, says us," We sang as we worked cribbing Robert Louis Stevenson's song. Our Ruesga camp became livable again though we'd have to wing it for the remainder of that summer in our toy town tent, and have to flee again to Mercedes' at the first drop of rain.

"Had enough of living in a tent? Anyone want to give up?" Ed questioned jokingly over comida at the Juanon later that afternoon.

Greeted by a hail of not mes, he broke into a smile. "Who votes we camp here next year and every summer for years and years?"

"Me. Me. I want to," Anthony replied.

"I want to, too," Miles agreed.

"And me. I'm in," I answered. "But on one condition. We buy real tents. Brand new ones with proper flysheets from a sports shop."

"And, one more thing….," I paused,

"We dig a ditch around the tents," we chorused.

The villagers' attitude towards us changed after that. Made us one of them. Little gifts, a bulb of garlic, a head of lettuce, an onion appeared outside our tent. An acknowledgment we were human and no different from them. Curious to see me on my knees chopping, cooking, women passing by on their way to and from the meadow slowed their pace.

"*Buenas tardes*," they called.

8

OUR PALACIO DE ALGODON YEARS

The English are coming, hurrah, hurrah,
The English are coming, hurrahaah.

A kind of homecoming ritual, unable to contain ourselves, the song rang from the open window as we turned onto the last stretch of road before Ruesga.

Just two kilometers remained. Ed leaned on the horn tooting in time with our voices and calling out familiar landmarks as they came into sight, our excitement mounting. Triggered memories cascaded.

"Look, the Almonga," we chorused spotting the familiar outline of granite above the village.

"Look, that's Aquilino's field where we helped him load his hay, and there's the stand of chopos where we played hide-n-seek behind their trunks, and ooh, remember riding Alejandro's cow, Miles?"

Then with one last turn of the steering wheel across the bridge before us lay Ruesga. Our village.

Perfectly timed, standing in the river shallows where the Pisuerga widened to a tranquil pool, a small herd of village cows froze in the act of drinking to stare at us as if they'd been waiting the full year for our return.

"Isn't that Aurora, Maria's daughter from the Upper Bar minding them? My, she's grown," we waved. Motionless, she stared suspiciously as we drove passed.

Next moment Anthony and Miles tumbled out of the car and ran to hurl themselves into Mercedes' skirts as she came running to greet us.

"*Bienvenidos mis bribones. Ayee, como ha creceden.*"

Clasping her "little rascals" to her, Mercedes exclaimed how much they'd grown, laughingly pinching their arms and cheeks, she held them at arms' length before finally releasing them.

"*Ven. Ven. Um vaso primero. Juan todovia trabajando. Pero viene pronto y ayudar-te. Ven. Ven. Ahora hablamos.*"

She sat us down in the kitchen while we waited for Juan to return from the fields. To get to work and set up camp before he arrived was out of the question after last year's fiasco. I couldn't speak for smiling. Mercedes kept tight hold of my hand alternately patting and kissing it as we sat together round the table swapping news while we waited.

Everything as before, looking round, I sighed. Herbs hanging from the beams, the smell of *jamon* curing over the wood stove, a brown enamel pot of beans simmering, the smoke-blackened beams. Home. Yes, I was home.

"*Miré...Juan llega,*" and there, filling the doorway stood her bear of a husband.

"*Holá,*" he beamed and clapped Ed across the back with such force he staggered. "*Venga,*" he said simply inclining his head for us to follow.

Faint indents in the meadow grass showed the exact spot where we pitched our toy town tent the year before. Still there, the patch of nettles with its clump of dock leaves growing along the base of the grey stone wall, the apple orchard, the line of poplars, *chopos*, marking the river course, the expanse of meadow and the Almonga's towering mass. Relief. Nothing had changed. We were back home. For evermore it seemed. Then.

Wordlessly, and with a swing of his mattock Juan set about gouging four drainage channels round each tent. They'll not flood again. Not if I have anything to do with it, I could see him thinking.

Biting back the forbidden thank-you, Ed pulled the cork of a brandy bottle and offered it to Juan. This was Spain, and when in Spain… I watched Juan take a token swig. Remembered I'd rarely seen him drink. So different, the two men. Juan, deeply tanned and arms the width of my thighs, then Ed, scrawny as an alley cat who lived by night from the look of his pasty, London pallor.

"*Entonces, me voy.*" Disappearing through the gate, Juan was gone leaving us to unpack.

With each saucepan, kettle, tarp, sleeping bag and folding chair pulled from our purple mini, the past grey months evaporated.

"We're here. We're here," I laughed kicking off my shoes and rolling in the cool meadow grass alongside the children.

"That's more like it. We'll be snug as four bugs in these," Ed admired tapping the blue flysheet covers sheltering our new tents. "No need for umbrellas over our sleeping bags like last year's Toy-town tent fiasco."

"Remember…? Remember Anthony and Miles?" I laughed with them recalling the night of torrential rain that forced us to flee.

The word was out. The English foreigners had arrived. Juanco, Juan's son appeared. Alejandro next, then his brother Ignacio followed closely by one-eyed Leandro as always in dark glasses. One by one, they, and other men friends of Ed's swung by to share a glass of wine, and bear hug one another with back-slapping clouts.

"*Bienvenidos.*" Genuinely pleased to see us they welcomed in turn.

"*Que Bueno. Mejor. Mas fuerte. Mas grande.*" Fingering the canvas, the guy ropes and peering inside our upgraded twelve by twelve-foot new summer home, each man murmured his approval.

"*Palacio de Algodon,*" Leandro pronounced. "Palace of Cotton," the name stuck.

Not yet adjusted to Spanish time, our greetings over, I wanted Alejandro and his pals gone. Unopened boxes of canned goods, suitcases of clothes and camping paraphernalia lay in untidy piles on the grass behind them. Thankfully milking time called and put an end to our welcome party.

By the time we got our air beds pumped, the fire pit built, and camp organized enough for the fast-approaching night, Almonga's shadow already blotted the daylight from the meadow.

"This is heaven on earth. I'm so happy to be back," I said sliding my arm around Ed's waist.

Slow-walking the earth-packed lane later to the Juanon, sights and smells, sounds and feelings dormant since the previous summer each tiny detail nudged me alive reminding me of all I'd missed. The sweet grass scent of cow patties filled my nostrils. In the traffic-free quiet, not even a footfall assailed my ears.

In the bar that first evening, we were taken aback by the sight of strangers trespassing our terrain.

"*Holá*," we said eying each other as they continued to their rooms, and we to the bar.

"City people," I dismissed, making a face. "I wonder what the devil they're doing here."

"What happened to the road builders from Galicia?" I questioned Mercedes when I saw her next.

"Long gone. Finished the project and returned home. Leandro's cousins and their seven children from Madrid have taken the Juanon for the whole summer," she explained. Little did we know it then, they would become lifelong friends.

That night cocooned in my sleeping bag I scanned the Milky Way's crowded galaxies imagining other beings gazing down to where I lay on earth, like me, I imagined wondering at our existence, and whether we grew wings or bombs. The unaccustomed cool breath of night on my face, the soft snores from my boys' tent, and the promise of warm summer months ahead, kept me awake long after Ed fell asleep.

I woke to the confusing scent of meadow grasses and wild flowers and a tapping sound above my head I couldn't at first place. A thrush? A blackbird? No way to tell, and I lay transfixed tracking a bird's three-toed silhouette hopping across the outer canvas until it flew away.

Careful not to disturb Ed, I slipped my feet into a pair of dry canvas espadrilles, untied the orange tent tabs and stood a moment in the opening, reluctant to step into the cool dew-soaked grass. Faint mewling cries from above me made me scan the sky to locate their source. Up they swept, two arcs of wingspan dark against the mist, I watched a pair of eagles, till they disappeared into the blue-pink shroud still lingering around the Almonga's crest.

Tilting the flagon of spring water, I filled and propped the blackened kettle on the firestones and sat back on my heels waiting for the snap-crackle sound of the starter twigs to tell me they were alight.

Fingers wrapped around my mug of tea listening to dawn's chorus watching the slow lift of the morning's haze reveal my meadow paradise. I reveled in this special hour. The time it gave me to not think, but to allow. To feel and set my day. I heard, before I saw, a flock of swallows swoop low over the field of wildflowers.

9

MY ROCK

Harvest safely gathered in, and our work in the fields with our friends finished for the day, one week remained. I prodded the smoldering embers pushing away thoughts of grey winter days to come, and the impending return to London's rigid routine.

Camping suited me. The slow routine. The connection to the earth. The time it gave me to unravel tangles from corners of my brain I'd been unaware of. My unconscious way, I realize now, of escaping the unpredictable pattern of my London life. Ed's altered mood after an evening's boozing with his Cockney mates. The warning fumble of his key in the lock. The narrowing of his eyes. The way we instinctively sprang apart when he saw me on the sofa, my arms around my boys. Our marriage unraveling. I was confused.

But in Spain, in our tiny Ruesga, for two summer months we fell in love again. In Spain for two summer months, Ed became a loving step-dad to my sons. In Spain they had a father and loved Ed back.

Each evening, when the sun lay low in the sky, I made it my habit to get supper going ahead of time. Ed happy sipping wine in the bar, and Anthony and Miles off running with their Spanish friends, once the orchard gate creaked shut and the last of the women still digging the evening's vegetables disappeared, the meadow became mine alone.

A wristwatch had no place for me in Spain, where Ruesga's days were governed by the heavens and our stomachs. I'd long given up my British insistence on punctual meals and early bedtimes as I had those earlier years. When in Spain… I reasoned. Aromas seeping from the simmering pot over the wood ash would announce supper ready.

Not quite day, not quite dusk, no deadline by which to lay the fire, prep the food, and get the cooking underway, I liked to settle on the log beside the fire pit and sit bare-toed doing nothing but listen to the shadows creeping through the meadow grass, and to stories whispered by the apple leaves in the orchard. No matter whether minutes, or perhaps an hour passed before I stirred.

Gathering a handful of still yellow broom, stick by stick, I snapped each brittle stem in two releasing heady scents of hillside, and arranged them over the ashes.

From the first strike of match and wisp of smoke to its greedy crackle, staccato thoughts calmed. I pulled loose a long and sturdy branch from our woodpile and pushed the thickest end into the flames to create a slow-burning orange glow.

"Like this," our friend Ulpiano had gently guided me a while back.

I smiled at the memory, how he and Juanna found me struggling to cook our supper over an open fire without burning the food to a crisp.

"Excellent cordon-noir. Yum," Ed mocked at the blackened meals I served.

Thick end for simmering, thin end for a fast boil, Ulpiano had shown me how to manipulate the flames and control the heat, so my one-pot dishes came out cooked to perfection. Rabbit, quail, chicken, lamb, a handful of vegetables and herbs, no meal repeated quite the same.

Ulpiano's teaching sang in my head.

Pulling back the wood, I let the fire die to a glow.

"That should do it," I thought aloud. "Time to begin my alchemy."

A splash of oil, pinch of spice, sprigs of herb, and dribble of wine, I intoned dropping in the main ingredients with a giggle.

Mistress of my kitchen, I wore the crown of a gypsy queen roaming the country in a caravan. A romantic fantasy not shared by all, I discovered.

Back a week or two before, Ed and I were driving Alejandro to Aguilar de Campo to stock up on wine from a particular bodega he'd heard about, when I discovered his darker side.

"Look gypsies just like us," I pointed overtaking a small caravan of Travelers on the road.

At the word gypsy, Alejandro's face had twisted into a snarl. The hatred in his voice murderous. I looked at him askance wondering at the inferno bubbling beneath his normally placid demeanor.

"*Non. Non,*" Alejandro raged, "*Gitanos, malos.*"

I turned for a closer look. Plodding peaceably, a lone donkey harnessed in front, the group of disheveled, barefoot children and three donkeys roped behind a house on wheels no larger than a hen's nesting box were hardly a threat.

"They're just hungry and tired, needing a place for the night." I swallowed the words I was about to say. No arguing with that man.

What would he have called me, I wondered, half-remembering my own childhood journeys, the endless string of homes in which I lived before my seventh Birthday. Bungalow to bungalow, bed to bed, by car, bus, open lorry and train even huddling one sleepless night on the platform of a crowded Indian railway station sandwiched inside a bedding-roll between my little brother and mother. I supposed Ernie, Ed's full-bloodied gypsy friend, would have despised us too. Traveler. Hedge-bumper. I could hear him sneer.

"*Cabrónes. Ladrones.*" Alejandro spat expletives through the window.

Leaning back in my folding chair I lazily scanned the meadow's play of greens, striped earth tones, the line of pale willows marking the riverbank. Beside me in the deep shadowed slope of the Almonga, a ladybird landed on my foot.

Humming, I scooped the vermillion spotted creature onto my palm and freed it to the sky.

Supper prepared and simmering on the fire pit, the blackened pan capped, its lid weighted with a heavy stone safe from hungry dogs, I headed for the lone rock a good half-hour's walk away. The rock I claimed as my special place, the place where I could breathe. Almost impossible to pick out from the village, its grey mass crouched, clawing the mountainside waiting for me just above the tree line.

Dawdling, I nibbled my way across the meadow, pausing every few steps to sample each variety of leaf and flower. Though I traveled this meadow path more times than I could count, I swear the earth itself offered up a treasure each time I passed. A sliver of vole jawbone, still with its row of tiny ivory needle teeth in place caught my eye. I stooped to pick it up and slipped it into my pocket.

Crawling through the fence, I made for the narrow gap in the blackthorn hedge. However carefully I tried, I never made it through without its barbs scoring at least a couple of bloody scratches.

Oh…what…a…beee…uti…full…day, I pursed my lips whistling soundlessly in rhythm with each panting step up the steep slope. I climbed slowly. Ran my tongue over my lips. Wished I'd brought water.

The trees thinned to scrub. At last. There it was, the lone lump of granite, my look-out post rooted in the meadow grass.

Clambering up the rock's rough face I flopped down, kicked off my canvas shoes and surveying my domain, traced the path I'd hiked from our village campsite to reach my private space. Still out of breath, a mighty sigh escaped me as, like an eagle peering from its eerie, I noted every little thing I saw and heard. A faint murmur of Gusto's voice and ninnying chorus of his goats and sheep floating from the village made me turn head to watch his flock—a surging, pitching tidal wave of black and brown—tumble through the narrow gorge of Ruesga's red-roofed buildings, then vanish into courtyards invisible from the street. Quiet settled. Nothing moved.

From darker shadows I made out the lane dissecting the village idly tracing its passage from Gusto's, the sheepherder's house near Maria's bar, down to the Juanon, and along the lane to our tents in Mercedes' meadow

A movement caught my eye. One behind the other, I idly watched two figures in peasant-black stoop and straighten along a furrow in the meadow. La Madre and her daughter, Manuella. Even from this great distance I could identify the women. Not from their faces, nor from their black dresses, did I recognize them, for all women in the village were uniformly clothed in widow's weeds, I knew them from the Anton's strip of meadowland they dug, the land their family had owned since the first settlers first peopled the valley more than a hundred years back.

The sun's bite softened. I pulled off my bra, and hitching up my dress rolled it furtively to my chin. Hair fanned flat across the rock, a velvet expanse of belly exposed, like a snake when released of his too tight skin, I wriggled my shape into the patch of soft moss carpeting. Drowsy, my eyes released their focus and thoughts not yet willing to be formed, drifted past carried on the evening's scented breeze.

As the last rays of day slipped behind the Almonga, a cloud of gnats settling on my face irritated me to full consciousness. Suddenly chilled, I buttoned my frock while madly swatting the air with my sunhat, and leaped from the rock to be rid of them. Then as suddenly as they arrived, forming a ball, the insects rose in the air and rolled over my head towards the reservoir.

Arms waving to keep my balance, I bounded from grass clump to clump chasing my lengthening shadow down the hillside and into the forest's maze of dark trunks, and speckled shade. My shadow was gone. Gobbled by deep shade.

A head of garlic, and two sweet white onions propped against the tent flap, welcomed me back. A thank-you from whom I wondered. Sometimes a head of cabbage, a bundle of green beans or whatever was surplus…I often found little gifts. A token for helping in the fields, for being their friend, for no reason at all but sharing.

The aroma of spiced chicken seeping from the simmering pot

on the ashes, told me supper was fully cooked. Lifting the lid, I sniffed the dish and checked the gravy's seasoning before setting off to gather the boys, and join Ed and his friends.

Ed, holding forth at Juanon's Lower Bar, waved and continued talking.

"*Holá*, Isabel," his buddies called. No longer silenced by my presence, when I, a woman, entered, his buddies briefly acknowledged me before turning back to Ed.

"*Holá*. Supper's ready when you are, Ed." I announced joining him, praying he wouldn't be much longer.

10

HARVEST TIME

As harvest approached, Alejandro spoke of nothing but. Twice, three times a day he stared at his fields, rechecking for the green tinge coloring the hillside to ripen to gold.

"Only once the crop failed," he related. "Too much rain. La Madre was forced to beg grain and flour from the miller in exchange for costly *pesetas*."

In the short window of harvest, Ruesga's normally sleepy lanes erupted with soft thunk of cowbells and crunch of rolling carts. Unhurried, cows still plodded, women prepared meals, and men took time to down a *vino* or two at the bar. But I could feel a shift, the raring to begin, the urge to be the first family to bring in the crop.

"Is the crop ripe yet? Hot enough?" Caught up in his anxiety, we too, pestered Alejandro, scanning the sky, the yellowness of the oats.

I don't remember how our working with Alejandro's family came about, if we just attached ourselves to him without asking that third year, or if Ed turned up one day at his field above the village and asked Alejandro to show him how to fork, load, and unload the carts.

Ed was the first to volunteer. Not from obligation. We turned up when and if we wanted. Late mornings and evenings mostly, to avoid the heat. At first, the boys and I tagged along just for the fun of being in the open air, and for the bumpy cart ride. But by watching, then helping, we began to help as well. Little things like raking, or just holding still the cows.

"*Holá, professor,*" Ed greeted Alejandro with the honorific title he'd crowned him, "*Que trabajo hoy, jefe?* What work today, boss?" At which Alejandro cracked a smile inclining his head towards the area he'd been working and wordlessly handed Ed one of his hand-worked forks from the back of the wooden cart.

July and into the first week of August, every day followed the same pattern once the harvesting was under way. Field by field, load by load, late afternoons when the bite of the sun no more than nibbled, the family stripped the hillside of every golden stem. Extra panels fitted to both sides of the cart held the mountain of grain we'd just harvested in place. With much laughter one of the men often gave Anthony and Miles a leg-up for the ride home. I could just make them out, half buried by the loose, flat on their tummies, their two smiling faces peering down at us from the top of the load. Not a smooth ride. Sometimes swaying dangerously, the cart lurched down the rocky lane to *la Era*. The end of their work day in sight, the men soon had the load forked and spread into an untidy *corona* so it could dry overnight.

Most days we presented ourselves to help out. No obligation, we turned up when, and if, we felt like and for no reason other than he was our friend. No please, no thank you, it was enough for us to see Alejandro's half smile when we appeared. During harvest when every hand was needed, a trip to the upper fields became a family affair: Alejandro, his brother Ignacio, when he was still alive, Manuella his sister, her husband Mariano and often as not, Ulpiano and Juanna, their cousins from the nearby town of Cervera. Plus, us of course. Four tag-alongs, we followed wherever the cart lead us.

I'd not felt as healthy for years. Proud of their firmness, I squeezed my hardened biceps. I flexed my muscles. Sun burst from my veins. My skin smelled of meadow flowers. Spring water purer than wine slaked my thirst. And each night I flew on the back of an owl.

Waking from siesta one afternoon late July we looked in on Alejandro and found him, his brother, Ignacio, and their sister Manuella in his *quadro* in party mood assembling an assortment of scythes, forks, rakes, and bisoms.

"Come to get your hands dirty, eh?" Ignacio joshed, clearly pleased to see us. Alejandro too, though a clap on Ed's back and a nod was his only acknowledgment.

"*Merienda. No olvides,*" La Madre called appearing at the doorway, a lumpy cloth bundle clutched to her chest for them to take to the fields. "*Manuella. Toma por arriba.*"

"*Hup. Hup, La Reina. Adelante, Tesuga,*" scattering a cloud of flies from around their eyes with a shake of their heads, the cows strained at the yoke and set the cart moving.

Alejandro ahead, the cows in his footsteps, then Ignacio and Manuella with the four of us following, our jolly procession headed for the stony lane and over the bridge to the far side of the river. This was fun. The work of important Generals. Anthony and Miles marched behind the cart each with a stick-gun over their shoulder.

Ignacio made a lunge for Miles and lifted him squealing astride Tesuga's bony back. Without even a flick of her tail she plodded on unbothered by the extra burden. As the lane rose steeply the group fell silent. The only noise, the grind and scrunch of the cart's slow turning wheels.

I let the others pull ahead wanting the lane to myself. I paused to inspect a broken eggshell fallen from a nest. A smudge of yellow the only hint of the tiny life it once held, I peered into its void. A thrush's, I guessed from its scattering of tan speckles.

Hazel, blackthorn, honey suckle, and jagged-leafed dog rose fought for space in the towering hedgerows lining both sides of the lane. Grass and wildflowers dangled downwards from the undergrowth into my path, to touch me. Unwilling to pass the tiniest flower, I slowed pausing to smell, touch, count each petal. I struggled to pull the names from the recess of my brain. Tormentil. Stonecrop. Forget-me-not. Campion and…and… Then faster and faster, out the names tumbled: larkspur-cranesbill-speedwell-jack-in-the-pulpit-love-in-the-mist-primrose-meadowsweet. How could people call them weeds. The hedgerow vibrated. Spotting a shepherd's purse, I plucked a tiny heart-shape, split it open it with my thumb nail and marveled at its double row of pale seeds. Its magic money, I first discovered on my daily walks to school along the country lanes of Devonshire when I was eight.

"Boys. Boys. Come see." I looked up wanting to share my treasure with Anthony and Miles, but they were too far ahead to hear me.

The cart had halted I realized. Hoping they weren't waiting on me, I hurried to catch up with them. I found them staring at a wet patch of moss in the hedge one side of the lane.

"*Fuente,*" Ignacio pointed to the steady of water trickling from a narrow cleft between two rocks.

"*Bebe. Muy rico.*" Manuella held a handful to show me before gulping it down herself. She took a step back so I could have a turn, and wiped the dribbles from her chin with the back of her hand.

"Go on Mum. We've drunk some," Anthony encouraged.

Almost too icy, I drank its bubbling water from my cupped hands.

Almost at a crawl, the cows made the final slope and came to a standstill. The lane ended.

"*Aqui,*" Alejandro announced startling me. "*Mi campo.*"

"*Donde?*" I asked confused searching for the boundary line only he could see.

"*Miré. Este piedra,*" he pointed to an indistinguishable tussock of grass. "Mine here, Aquilino's there, and Juanillio's over there."

I shook my head. Ignacio and Manuella, brother, sister, settled on the grass in a patch of shade.

Alejandro reached into the rear of the cart for his scythe, and drew out the whetstone from the hollow of a goat's horn hanging from his belt. Upending the scythe, he sharpened the blade with deft strokes.

Instead of getting right to work in the field as I expected, lowering himself to the ground, he lay on his side and hammered what looked like a flat-topped railway tie upright into the earth.

"A *Pithar*," he stated simply.

Head tipped forward, hammer in hand, focused as I ever saw him, he serrated the scythe's blade.

"That's clever." I elbowed Ed admiring the row of jagged saw-teeth.

With a cautious test of his thumb, Alejandro approved its sharpness.

Maybe he was resting, perhaps planning which end of the field to tackle first, Alejandro stood staring over his crop. No village visible below. Ruesga's red roofs disappeared. A sea of standing grain stalks spread from horizon to horizon. Yellow. Shifting. But for a faint crackling rub of oats ears against one another, a sad sighing, no sound broke the silence.

"*Ahora. Ellos vienen,*" he said seeing Ulpiano y Juanna emerge from the lane.

"*Holá. Holá.* You mean you haven't even started yet and you're not finished by now?" Ulpiano, Mariano's cousin joked cheerfully.

Both no more than four feet tall, one plump, one thin, he and Juanna stood together bright-faced, inseparable.

Juanna's openness, and Ulpiano, with a smile equaled only by the broadness of his shoulders, and the blue badge of coal dust tattooed across his forehead from a mine accident that labeled him a coal miner, who couldn't love them both? So unabashedly joyous compared to every other Spaniard we'd met, I found myself laughing a lot when we were together. No wonder the four of us became such good friends.

Ulpiano may have been short, but I could tell from his muscular physique he had as much strength as Alejandro and Ignacio put together. Unabashed, he stripped to his singlet to expose a surprising forest of body hair. Always the joker, he mimed a classic strongman pose, bulged his biceps once, twice, three times, then strolled slowly to the cart and selected his scythe.

"*Listo,*" he announced.

No way to guess he'd already put in a full day's work underground hacking coal, Ulpiano stood ready to begin.

"*Aqui con nos otros.*" Alejandro signaled Ed and handed him a scythe. No instruction. No dos and don'ts or hint of how to use it.

"Seems I'm finally being allowed to do man's work." Ed commented over his shoulder as he walked away. "I've been wanting to have a go for ages."

In unison, three abreast, the men swung their blades at the tightly packed stems. Swing, step, swing, cutting low they carved deep swathes in the standing crop. Effortlessly in perfect arcs, the stalks fanned flat before Alejandro's and Ulpiano's feet. Not for Ed, poor sod. Six paces behind. Snared by tendrils of columbine, and roots, again and again, his scythe jerked him to a stop. I watched him struggle to keep up, tussle the blade-tip free from the earth. No word of criticism, Alejandro silently observed, watched the furrows across Ed's forehead deepen, his lips set tight with frustration, waited till Ed finally gave up and asked what the hell was he was doing wrong. Only then did Alejandro step in and demonstrate.

"*Si. Ahora.* Yes. Now!" Never correcting, allowing Ed to discover for himself, Alejandro commented only when Ed's swing looked right.

Half the field's golden stems lay felled. Forlorn, untidy jumbles littered the stubble. Gone the glorious carpet of oats.

Ignacio and Manuella dragged to their feet reluctant to begin the back-breaking work. Bent almost double, sickle in hand, I watched the two of them hook and gather great bundles from the ground, prop them upright forming rows of Pyramid-shaped…um…stooks. I recalled the obsolete word.

Thinking it our turn to get to work, I started to my feet to join them.

"*Sientate. Espere. Pronto. Necesario ellos avanzar um poco mas.*" Juanna motioned me to stay where I was until the men got a little further ahead. Though her Spanish was incomprehensible, I understood we had to wait.

With nothing yet for us to do, Juanna and I sat together resting in the shade. The late afternoon heat hung heavy. For a while I followed their progress counting the army of stooks forming behind them as they worked the field. Brother. Sister. Ignacio, with his one good arm and Manuella with her massive beam-end stuck in the air.

Ignacio was still alive then, for those first five years we summered in Spain. Reminiscing, I pictured his swarthy face, the dark unshaven stubble on his chin, the tail of his shirt pulled out, working the sickle's curved blade with his one good hand beside his brother.

My eyelids began to droop. Shadow leaves reflected from the hedge behind me patterned my legs and lap. A light breeze feathered my hair. I watched a grasshopper clinging to a blade of grass.

"*Ven Isabel.*" Juanna prodded me to the present handing me a spare rake. "*Ven,*" she called again.

Using its long handle to pull myself to standing, my hand slipped comfortable into the indentations whittled by the maker's knife.

"*Ver. Asi.* Look. Like this," she raked a pile of stray fronds, pointed, then stood back to watch me.

Gleaners. Our task was to finish up, winkle every seed of grain and yellow stalk from the stubble. One a little behind the other, a team, me raking, and she, with her bisom, sweeping.

Dreamily, I groomed each furrow. Treading lightly on the earth, I became aware only of the pull of wooden teeth, the lift and swing of my arms. I was the rake. I was the grain. I was each step I took. How simple my life would be if in my English life I focused on a single moment, just one thought, one footstep, and one worry at a time.

"*Merienda.* Time for a break," Manuella's loud call interrupted the calm.

Already? I'd barely been raking a minute it seemed.

The men, stretched out already on the ground, sat up when Juanna and I joined them in the slanting shade. Grouped together in a circle, our faces, clothes and limbs flecked with chaff and grit, we looked like a gathering of sunburned scarecrows. Talking, laughing all at once, our first Merienda de campo erupted into a party.

Manuella's plump legs stuck straight in front of her. A strand of dark hair peeked from her white headscarf and stuck to her temple. All eyes on her, we watched closely as slowly, oh so slowly, she untied the cloth bundle on her lap.

"*Manchego, jamon, y cecena,* special treat," she called unwrapping the food.

"Dried horse meat," I exclaimed revolted, hoping I could avoid trying it

"*Olé. Olé.*" Ulpiano held his *bota* at arms-length aiming the stream of wine directly into his mouth, then passing the leather bottle to Ed, encouraged him to do the same. Taking turns, the boys too, we gulped of the cool mix of diluted wine and gaseosa.

"*Non. Miré*," Ignacio vied to hold his bota the furthest distance from his body demanding our attention.

"*Para. Para*," Manuella gave him a mighty nudge knocking the stream of liquid down his chin.

"My. I can see your fingers through that slice," I exclaimed as a sliver of paper-thin Jamon fell from his knife. A fleeting smile cracked Alejandro's normally impassive face. Forty? Fifty? Whatever his age, I had no way of telling. His cheeks, his hazelnut skin as smooth as a newborn's gleamed from beneath his hat.

That's strange, I puzzled. "Alejandro usually wears a *boina*."

Sitting on the grass next to Manuella, Juanna pulled out a knife from the cloth bundle and attacked the round loaf of bread. Pressing the crust against her chest, using all her strength she pulled the knife-blade in a curve towards her and carved us each a hunk. One slip and… well, that didn't bear thinking about.

I looked around. Happy. If I had just one word to describe our group, yes, happy. I'd use happy.

11

LA ERA

In the quiet of the setting sun, I looked back to the denuded field behind us. Scythed, raked and devoid of single ear of grain, only stubble remained. The boys and men ahead with the cart, I lingered behind our little caravan as it creaked slowly home.

Loose strands of oats snatched from the overladen cart, and flattened wild flowers along both hedgerows marked its passage down the steep and narrow lane.

"Whoa, *Machina. Mas despacio, Tesuga.*" Alejandro tapped the yoke coaxing his cows to hold back.

Almost dusk, the last two still working on *la Era*, Alejandro and Ed swiftly unloaded the crop we'd just harvested from the upper field and spread it in an untidy circle to dry overnight.

While they finished up, I watched them, two shadowy men forking grain in the surreal landscape where I stood. Thrown as if by some giant discus player, a scattering of golden circles lay across the threshing floor reflecting the last of the light.

"*Bastante por hoy. Vamanos,*" Alejandro announced work over for the day and threshing would begin the next day after milking.

"Did you have any idea what Alejandro was talking about? Threshing sledge? *Trilla? Era?* Flints? *Corona.*" I asked Ed as we walked back towards the Juanon together.

"Not a clue. We'll find out soon enough," he replied.

Next morning Ed scuttled from the tent grabbing a hunk of bread and cheese as he hurried through the meadow gate.

"No time for breakfast. Alejandro's teaching me to how to *disparthia*, whatever that is," he called.

Already on *la Era*, Alejandro surveyed the crop the two of them had unloaded the previous evening. Dew-soaked, the crisp ears and stalks of yesterday lay limp and matted flat.

"*Buenas Professor. Aqui estoy,*" Ed saluted.

"*Primero voy a disparthia.*" Alejandro shook loose a soggy clump with his fork and tossed it to form a circle roughly thirty-feet in diameter. "The stalks have to dry out for a couple of hours."

Ed followed behind Alejandro. Stab, lift, shake, toss. The aerated grain rose high about his thighs.

"I'd really like to, Alejandro. Let me take over. I can do this on my own. This will be my job every day harvest lasts," Ed insisted.

Alejandro gave Ed a funny look, then nodded smiling. He stood a moment watching. Checking. Then raising his *bota* squirted a stream of cool *Rosado* into his mouth. Satisfied, he turned his back, and sauntered off.

Not every day, but sometimes, after the boys and I had finished our breakfast, I watched Ed *disparthia*. Not straining, as in a dance he moved in rhythmic steps slowly round the circle forking, lifting, fluffing. His London face erased, I saw him visibly soften in a way I'd not seen the past year.

"It's a meditation," he explained. "It makes me feel good."

Relaxed and the happiest we'd been since I couldn't remember when, we strolled together back our tent. The start of another gorgeous day, as with every morning, the sun shone, the sky arced flawless blue. Accustomed to grey clouds and damp, I never got used to the miracle.

"Who's for a swim? I'm stuck all over with chaff. How about it, boys? We've three hours at least before threshing begins." Ed disappeared into the tent to slip into his trunks and in less than a minute all four of us emerged decent with our legs hidden beneath regular clothes for the short stroll through the village to the lake.

Not a ripple, the water's surface seemed too perfect to disturb. I'd hardly dipped beneath the cool surface it seemed, when Ed's disembodied voice cut across the sparkling surface.

"Hey porpoise. We should be getting back."

I was getting into my work clothes at the tent, Anthony and Miles came tearing from *la Era* wild with excitement.

"Everyone's tobogganing Mum. Come and see."

"Really? Toboggans?" I looked at them askance.

"Yes. Truly. Truly."

They were right. Nothing could have prepared me. *La Era* teemed with sledges circling the threshing floor. I just stood and stared.

Not a single machine in sight...wooden sledges, milking cows shod with iron shoes, hand fashioned yokes bound with leather, rakes, and farming tools unchanged for perhaps two thousand years, I'd been dropped into another century. Neighbor beside neighbor, each family working their separate *coronas*, almost the entire village had gathered for the first day of threshing. Men, women, children, cows, calls and boisterous laughter, the normally empty Era buzzed with activity.

"Better find Alejandro," Ed nudged me.

Half in and half out of a small shed, squeezed side by side in the cramped space, the two brothers struggled to manhandle what I assumed was a sledge into the open.

Propping the curious platform downside up, Ignacio and Alejandro rested a minute to catch their breath.

"*Pesado. Falta uno mas.*" Ignacio panted peeling away a couple of dusty spider webs from his hair and arms before once more disappearing with his brother into the shed's dim interior to fetch the second sledge.

"*Un Trilla, Trilliar*," Alejandro annunciated slowly giving me a new noun, threshing sledge, and then the verb to add to my vocabulary.

I walked around the object studying its approximate five-foot platform curved upwards ski-like at the front, the planks formed an even surface wide enough to hold a chair. And from its underside, I was startled to see closely spaced rows of flint stones jutting from its surface.

"Do you mean to tell me that...?" My voice trailed. I caught my foolish question in time and reached to touch one. Razor-sharp, I quickly retracted my hand and checked whether I was bleeding.

White, brown, sienna, all shades of greys and black, their earth colors against the blonde wood made the sledge look like a piece of art rather than a tool.

Fingering the empty spaces, Ignacio ran his withered hand between the rows pausing now and then and hammering in a replacement to fill the gap.

"Do you make these yourself, Ignacio?" I quickly retracted my hand and checked whether I was bleeding.

"No, I get them from a stone napper in Reinosa. But this year, I have enough. *No importa este ano, tengo bastante*." Ignacio shrugged and wandered off with his brother to bring up the cows, Ed trailing with them.

Glad to have a moment alone, I settled on the cropped grass to absorb a scene I couldn't imagine still existed in the 1960's. One. Two...I counted eleven separate family threshing floors. Not a combine harvester in sight, half buried in the grain, *la Era* heaved with pairs of plodding cows hauling sledges round each *corona*.

After the earlier chaotic first-day-excitement subsided, *la Era*, had settled, calmed to a hypnotic ocean of ceaseless movement.

Filtering the scene through half-closed lids it was easy to imagine the bow of a rowboat nosing through waves, and the sound of the tide pulling back from a beach. Eyes closed, I heard the sigh of the sea, the hiss of wood sliding over grain. There on the threshing floor of that small village in the Spanish mountains, one hundred miles inland from the coast, I heard it.

"*Holá*," Maria plonked herself down, not beside, but almost on my lap.

She leaned against me sideways. Her skirted thigh too hot against mine in the August heat, her thickly stockinged legs too scratchy, she stuck them into the sun like two felled tree trunks and pinned me next to her.

"*Miré. Ellos viene con los vacas. Ordeño terminado.*" Removing a length of straw from between her front teeth to speak, Manuella broke the silence with a sudden dig of her elbow in my ribs.

"*Bueno.*" I scrambled to my feet grateful for the excuse to escape.

Milking over, the five of them appeared, Ignacio and Alejandro each leading a pair of cows yoked together and ready for work, Ed following with a couple of rakes and wooden forks slung over his shoulder, and Anthony and Miles staggering under the weight one of La Madre's kitchen chairs.

We watched Alejandro attach the sledge to Tesuga's and Estrella's yoke, while Ignacio hitched La Machina and Romera to the second. With an occasional stamp of a hoof and swishing of tails to drive off the flies, the two pairs stood calmly in front of each sledge placidly chewing their cud. Half hidden under dangling fringes of fur draped over their heads, I could barely make out their eyes.

"Are those legs?" I exclaimed aghast looking closely at the fringes.

"*Si. Perros,*" Alejandro answered matter-of-factually.

"Dog's?" I'd shrieked. "Why dog's?"

"*Las moscas odian el olor,*" he explained wrinkling his nose. Ah, so that's why the flies keep away.

"*Y,*" he continued, "*el piel del ellos están el mejor. El yugo no frotando con esto.*" He pointed to the yoke where the dogskin protected Tesuga's neck.

Who was I to interfere? I swallowed and turned away.

"*Tiempo. Vamanos,*" and with an *adelante-ven*, both pairs waded into the sea of grain and began circling in opposite directions to each other. Apart from an occasional *Hup-Hup-Arre*, Alejandro and Ignacio let the cows alone. The cows knew the drill so well, Alejandro and Ignacio had little to do but sit and wait till the long stems shortened to lengths of straw and the ears of grain lay severed on the ground.

12

THRESHING FUN

One *corona* over, next to Alejandro's where we were gathered, Leandro skimmed by standing balanced on his sledge, legs apart as if he surfed a golden sea. Mostly villagers like Maria from the Upper Bar threshed from the comfort of a chair. I would never have expected to see Maria working on *la Era*. But there she was, her cheeks faintly pinked from unaccustomed sunshine, lounging on a wicker basket chair driving a sledge. Relaxed, looking almost girlish in a white headscarf wrapped forties-style around her head, I watched her lean forward and gently encourage her pair of cows. Catching sight of my Brownie Box Camera pointed at her, she coyly smiled as she glided by.

"Can I? Can I?" Not waiting for Alejandro's answer, Miles waded through the waist-high stems and leaped in front of Alejandro and sat between his knees pretending to drive. Round and around, circling in the opposite direction to the other sledge, he looked utterly absorbed. I wondered what thoughts roamed in my child's head, what role Miles played in his imagination that he looked so dreamy, so happy.

Reflecting, I sat with Manuella in the thin strip of shade waiting for the *corona* to flatten, and the long stems shorten sufficiently so we could rake.

I turned to watch Anthony. Standing alone, I could see from his expression he longed to take part. I was about to call him over when Ignacio beat me to it.

"*Ven. Tonio. Ven con migo,*" Ignacio beckoned.

In a flash Anthony hopped across the *corona* and settled on Ignacio's lap. For a couple of circuits that's all they did, just sit and watch allowing Anthony to take everything in. Then lightly tapping Anthony's shoulder to get his attention, Ignacio, mimed and gestured how to control the cows.

"Okay?" Ignacio queried signing a thumbs up, and handing Anthony his stick jumped from the sledge leaving him to steer on his own.

Hat tipped forward, eyes shaded, stick in hand, his shirt half buttoned, Anthony slouched back in his chair as if he'd driven a team of cows his whole life.

"*Hup. Arre,*" I heard him call as he circled past.

How typical of Ignacio to make sure Anthony was included. I liked that about the man, about the people of Ruesga for treating my deaf son, and anyone disabled, the same as anyone else.

I pictured old, blind Angèl with his seeing-stick shuffling to and from the wall; incontinent Isabella, her skirt half buttoned wandering the village unrestrained searching for the life she'd mislaid; and fifteen-year-old Claudio with the mind of a toddler who never mastered speech.

I looked over to where the boy stood gurgling happily to himself while his mother worked. Rocking backwards and forwards, drooling a little, Claudio squinted at a piece of knotted string he liked to dangle in front of his eyes. Always together, his mother's shadow, clutching the hem of her apron I often came across the two of them in the lane.

I looked from him to my son. Anthony to Claudio. Part of the village, included in every activity, both had their place. I thought of the cruel reactions Anthony suffered back in England, and tears sprung to my eyes.

"*Eh Milo. Prisa. Prisa. Milo. Mierda estropea la paca.*" Alejandro jabbed him to the present as he saw Estrella lift her tail. Quickly snatching up the battered enamel chamber pot beside him he shoved it into Miles' hand.

"Quick Miles. Catch the shit before it fouls the crop." Ed and I chorused, laughing at the face he made. "Well caught Mister-patty-catcher. That's your job now, so it's up to you to keep an eye out."

The excitement over, I sat with Manuella in the shade of the shed waiting for our turn to rake. Over the next hour, I noticed the long stems becoming shorter lengths with each circuit, and seeds of grain littered the ground. Miles was happily working. Anthony too. I jumped to my feet with a sudden urge to ride a sledge.

"Anthony. Anthony," I waved to attract his attention. "Me. Me," I pointed, "I want a go."

I lasted all of a minute. The minute I sat on the chair, those devil cows veered off the circle and headed for home. Jeering with laughter, Ignacio and Anthony jumped to my rescue, and got them back under control.

On hour passed. Half its original height, the outer rim of the flattened *corona* spilled untidily out of shape.

Surely, Manuella and I could do something now?

As if reading my thoughts, Manuella bent and scooped a handful of grain trapped in the grass. She mimed sweeping then pointing to my chest.

"*Pero, primero arreglarse,*" she instructed handing me a rake and then one to Ed indicating he should work the outer rim.

Eager to show off, I wasn't completely useless, I waded behind Manuella to the center of the circle, and bounded into action speed-raking the straw. Foolish of course. In less than ten minutes, completely puffed out and sweating, I had to rest. Not Manuella.

Not her, she knew how to pace her movements and keep going all day-long. I stood admiring her rhythmic swing, her unhurried step, the steady way she worked.

Step, rake, breathe. Step, rake, breathe.

Taking up my rake once more, I swung my arms and twisted my hips imitating her dance. Working so slowly felt unnatural at first, lazy even. Then, getting into the rhythm of it, I tuned in to the hiss of polished wood skimming grain, and saw and heard as never before. Mmm, I hummed. Mmm, I inhaled... sweet smelling cud, the crunch of cow shoes snapping straw, the blend of human and animal's sweat. This was life. One with nature. No telephones, no machines. The life I wanted to give my children.

I caught Manuella watching me. Did she read my mind? She smiled her approval.

All across *la Era*, women doing women's work, men doing men's. No argument. No questioning. Surprisingly, I discovered I liked the Spanish order of things, their traditional division of roles, of being honored as a woman.

Manuella and I stood for a moment, idly watching the still circling sledges. The morning's thick disc of un-cut stems had been reduced to a mere ring on the outer edge.

"Hmm. *Corona,* crown," I mused. The name made perfect sense.

"It's a good life," I announced in English nudging her.

She turned to stare at me not understanding a word, then nodded a little surprised.

"*Listo? Ahora barremos.*" Manuella handed me a bisom of broom she'd harvested from the surrounding hills.

I looked at the bunch of dried twigs tightly bound with wire in disbelief.

"What, you want me to sweep the grass?" I almost laughed. "With this?"

But it worked. And efficiently too, leaving barely a grain between the stubby blades. Bent nearly double, the sun grilling through the cotton of my blouse, we swept and we swept that circular threshing floor from the middle out, till not a kernel of grain remained.

"*Bastante,*" Manuella called signaling enough with her hands.

The sun already past its zenith, we'd been threshing for nearly three hot hours and I was about done. I watched Alejandro and Ignacio un-hitch their cows, and prop the sledges against the side of the little shed. And I made ready to head back.

"*Donde vas Isabel?*" One last job remained to do before lunch.

I turned to see Alejandro and Ignacio hitch a curious long handled wooden object I can only liken to a giant window wiper blade to the yoke of the strongest pair of cows.

"*Ven. Ven. La ayuda de todos.*" Everyone needed, they beckoned. "*Saltamos.*"

"Jump on Isabel. They need all our weight," Ed translated.

Ignacio and Manuella jumped onto the long wooden blade, then Ed, the boys, and a couple of neighbor's kids followed, all of us fighting for footholds on the inch-wide edge.

"This is crazy," I laughed grabbing the back of Ed's and Ignacio's belts. From somewhere beneath the pile of bodies, I could hear Anthony and Miles giggling.

"All of you okay? Hold on for dear life." Ed called over their heads.

Somehow, I found a space to squeeze my toes just as the cows lurched forward. Gathering speed they careened across the *corona* dragging us and the horizontal wooden blade behind them scraping the grain and straw into a cone shaped *monton* till it stood at least seven feet high.

"*Adelante. Adelante.*" Alejandro encouraged his cows.

"*Olé. Olé,*" we hollered, egging them on.

It wasn't just us, the whole Era had gone crazy scaping the straw and grain into a heap. Charging cows, laughter and shrieks, as a mass of bodies jumped on and off and were thrown from the scrapers. It would be the same the following day, the day after that and every day for at least the two weeks threshing lasted. One day's work, one monton. Cones of gold mushroomed beside each *corona* across *la Era*.

The higher the cone grew, the more difficult it became for the cows to drag the crop up the steep slope to the top forcing us all to leap for our lives or be thrown. Straw in our hair, straw on our clothes, we tumbled onto the straw-littered ground and rolled out of the way. I locked eyes with my sons, sharing laughter as we rarely did in our London lives with Ed around.

At last, the day's fun over, tired out and happy we headed to the bar for drink and a very late lunch.

Later back at camp, cozy around the fire, we sat reminiscing about our first day's threshing on *la Era* and began to laugh all over again.

"New words to add to our vocabulary," Ed said

"*Corrrrrona*," we trilled for *corona*.

"*Trrrrilla, Trrrrrillar*, for threshing sledge and to thresh. We rolled the unfamiliar *rrrr* with our tongues.

"Um. Um. Scraper-thing," we giggled finally, for not one of us recalled its name nor the verb used to describe its use.

13

THE BELLADORA ARRIVES

Kneeling on the grass outside my tent I glanced up from the soapy ash-flecked water of my washing up bowl, and paused. The meadow sounded, even looked different. No sign of Theodora, Manuella or the other women, no bustle, holàs or calls to welcome the day. Usually busy by this time of morning, I made out just one lone figure in the meadow. La Madre. I swilled out the last mug in the rinsing water, and propped it upside down on a rock..

The old lady hovered, stooping every now and then to pull a handful of white-bulbed onions from her vegetable patch. Black headscarf, dress and shawl-like wings, from this distance she could be mistaken for a raven pecking at a kill. I held my breath wishing I could freeze-frame the pastoral scene, the round hump of her as she worked, the contrast of her form stark against the sunlit backdrop of greens and browns. Tugging free the green shoots, she beat off clumps of magenta earth before tossing them into the willow basket beside her.

Dishcloth in hand, I gazed at the scene inexplicably overcome with a deep joy I couldn't name and burst into song.

My soul doth magnify the lord and my spirit doth re...jo...oi...oi...oi... rejoice in... The glorious notes of the Magnifica I'd once sung in Gloucester Cathedral shook the meadow.

A rumbling, metallic grinding, and cries from the lane beyond the meadow gate put an abrupt end to my solo. Tipping the soapy water into the hedge I tied shut the tent flaps as quickly as my fingers could manage and scurried down the lane and came upon a curious scene. Manhandling a squat, green wooden contraption the size of a half-grown elephant, Alejandro and Ignacio on one side, Manuella's husband, Mariano, and Ed the other, the four men strained to keep its wheels turning. Far too small, their iron rims racketed noisily on the uneven surface.

"Keep moving. *Adelante. Arre.*" Swishing her stick like a slave master, Manuella followed encouraging them in the same tone of voice she used for her cows.

More for the fun of it than to help, in and out and round again, Anthony and Miles and a small group of helpers dive-bombed between the weave of adult limbs like a cloud of gnats.

"*Empuje. Empuje.*" They yelped urging everyone to push.

"We're taking Alejandro's winnowing machine, to *la Era*. It's called a *Belladora*," Ed shouted over his shoulder as the group trundled past me. "Come on lazy bones. Give us a hand."

Not that my weight would make any difference, nor could I get close enough to be of any real use but to be a sport I squeezed into the melee. It took every ounce of effort to roll the unwieldy object the five hundred feet through the village and up the slight slope to *la Era*, but within a few minutes it had us gasping for breath. Still early, the lane lay mostly in shadow so at least the air felt cool.

Before making the final spurt we paused to catch our breath. I'd have given anything for a drink at that moment and eyed Alejandro gulp a cooling stream of *clarete* from his bota.

"Gasolina, or I die," I gasped wiping the sweat from my fore-head, and snatching the bota he offered me.

"Anyone...?

Mariano shook his head, and handed it on to Ed.

"*Arre. Bastante. Prisa. Las vacas necesitan ordenar,*" Manuella hurried us along to get back to milk the cows.

"*Uno. Dos. Tres. Olé. Olé...*" and with one wild charge, the heavy machine stood ready beside the family's *montons*.

Like ancient tumuli, mounds of grain stood grouped togeth-er beside Alejandro's and all the circular threshing floors scattered across the threshing floor. Maria's, boasted the most montons while Aquilino and other small families just three or four.

These six are ours, I thought proudly. One monton for each long day's work. Hard to believe this same straw and grain was a wav-ing sea of living oats in Alejandro's upper fields just a few days back.

Late as always, most families had already set up their *Belladoras* by the time our little troupe trundled into view. Leandro and his cousin, Nestor, stopped work to stare at us as we struggled by.

Mas fuerza en las castanetas, more strength in your balls, they jeered good-naturedly with vulgar country humor.

Ignacio countered with an up-your's gesture.

But with the dew not yet sucked from the montons of grain, and the *Belladora* safely parked and ready, there was nothing to do but wait. It would be an hour or two before the sun climbed higher in the sky for the crop to dry. Most villagers had already left *la Era* to milk the cows and attend to chores.

I had little energy that day despite dipping lazily in and out of the water for nearly two hours. By the time I sauntered up winnow-ing was well underway. Half the village, it seemed, crowded *la Era* that day but after the quiet of the reservoir, I felt I'd stumbled into a circus ring.

Noise and dust ballooning from every *Belladora,* I stared in hor-ror at the mayhem wondering whether to cover my ears or my nose or leave right then.

Directions flew. Alejandro's shouts mingled with the clatter and shudders of his and the other *Belladoras.*

"You and you—load. You and you crank the wheel...shovel... scoop..."

Already sweating, I had zero desire to exert myself in such heat and had to force myself to stay.

"*Holà*. Anything for me to do?" I asked praying I'd arrived too late.

If anybody heard, if anybody saw me, no one even bothered to look up. I flopped thankfully onto a shady spot by the shed, and pulled my straw hat down over my face to reduce the glare. To my amazement each space in its weave acted like a pinhole-camera sharpening people's features in a way I'd never noticed before. The blue of the sky deepened, the yellow of the grain. And I could even make out individual wisps of straw and blades of grass distanced from me. Like a scientist who'd made a remarkable discovery, I tested my observation. I lifted and replaced the hat from my eyes, disassembling, reassembling the focus. Off. On. Again and again.

As with every *Belladora* on *la Era*, people surrounded Alejandro's and every family's machine. Straw and dust flew, arms and forks jabbed the air at such a frenetic speed it seemed a whirlwind spun everyone out of control.

With *la Era* still wrapped in the heat of summer, and no sign yet of winter's coming, I wondered at the fevered work pace. No work. No food, yes that would keep me motivated. Absentmindedly picking a fallen grain of oat from the grass, I popped it into my mouth. Biting it in half, I spat out its outer husk and nibbled the chalky inside to a gluey paste wondering at the life contained within that single grain.

"Whatever are you doing? Come and help." Ed's shadow loomed above me. "At least come and watch what's going on."

"Okay. Okay. I'm coming," I said dragging to my feet.

I could just make out Ed and Alejandro under a cloud of chaff at the front end of the *Belladora* furiously harpooning bundles of oats from the monton into its gaping hopper. Straw and grit caked every sweaty body surface, and stuck to their clothes and berets. I held my breath and quickly skirted past them to the far side out of the dust and found Ignacio standing over Anthony and Miles.

Cranking the *Belladora*, their once scrawny city-boy arms, now bulged and tanned, blurred as they spun the handle together. The faster and faster their four hands cranked the wheel shuttling the three grids of graded mesh. Back and forth sifting the crop, gravel and sticks rattled through the largest mesh harmlessly onto the ground.

"*Mas rapido. Mas rapido,*" Ignacio egged them on shouting top volume over the fearful noise, till centrifugal force took charge sending the metal grids rattling back and forth so fast Anthony's and Miles' hands were thrown from the wheel forcing them to let go. The two of them collapsed out of breath and into such gales of laughter Ignacio had to take over.

Standing firm, turning the handle with his one good arm, Ignacio tilted his bronzed face towards Almonga's peak. Did he see his future? That this harvest would be his last, that never again would summer's sun darken his skin? It was our fourth year in Ruesga, the year before he died. The last time we worked beside him on *la Era*.

Walking further round, on the third side of the contraption, I stopped beside Manuella and Juanna and found them on their knees scrabbling grain like two terriers digging a hole. Side by side, heads close catching the unstoppable torrent of golden grain in a wooden trough, they filled sack after sack. Already six sturdy sacks as tall as my chest and full to the brim, stood behind the pile of empty sacks. Picking one up, I examined the rough weave of earth-brown and white goat hair. Patched and re-patched, the lengthwise stripes running top to bottom, somehow reminded me of the rows of bountiful furrows beyond our tent.

I was surprised to find Mariano at work beside the last chute. Heavily bandaged, and still in pain from an infection of the jaw that kept him closeted at home most of the summer, he'd clearly only emerged because Alejandro needed his help. Eyes scrunched against the flying dust, a red bandana over his nose and mouth, and his face wrapped like a mummy, he battled to trap the billowing clouds of chaff and straw into a massively wide sack. All at once he threw down his fork, clasped his bandaged jaw as if to stop it from falling off, and let out a sneeze so loud that Ignacio stilled the machine a moment to check if he was in trouble.

"*Olè. Olè. Jesus,*" we yelled as each successive sneeze exploded.

Hating at being singled out, Mariano sheepishly caught my eye with those translucent, underwater eyes of his, and smiled weakly. I felt bad for him. The man should be resting, I thought, not working in clouds of billowing chaff.

The very moment I had that thought, Ulpiano strolled up having just got back from full day's labor at the dark waterlogged coalface in Guardo the other side of the reservoir twenty miles from his home and then walked the two miles to Ruesga.

One look at his brother, and without being told, he gently prised the sack from Mariano and gesticulated he should go home. Used to being covered in coal dust, the flying chaff sticking to his shirt and face was nothing.

The clattering of the *Belladora* slowed and came to a stop. Winnowing was over and the harvest safely bagged.

"*Dieciseis.*" He stood proud counting and re-counting out loud. "*Bueno. Se acabo,*" Alejandro proudly poked each grain-crammed sack telling us harvest was done and finished. "Two sacks to the miller for flour. One extra to pay him, yes, we have more than enough for the year," he elaborated.

In a rare display of emotion, Alejandro's walnut face crinkled with delight forming cat's-whisker creases round his eyes.

Was that it? The harvest? Just those sixteen, those few sacks of grain? The family's reward for a whole year's labor? Was it possible for a family to survive on so little? I pictured my stuffed food cupboard back home and thought guiltily of my almost daily trips to the shops.

Sixteen. I admiringly fingered the rough wool tracing the brown and white stripes picturing the goat it came from.

"They're beautiful. I really like them. Who makes these?" I sighed.

"*Madre y jo. Hacemos en invierno.*" Manuella made a weaving action with her hands and pretended to shiver telling me they made them during the winter.

"*Toma. No vale por el grano.*" Manuella picked up an unused and useless, sack pitted with mice holes and offered it to me with a shrug.

"*Cabrónes ratones. Miré los pozos,*" she cursed poking her finger through one of the holes.

"*Ven a casa,*" Alejandro beckoned us to follow him home. "*Somos familia ahora.*"

I really did feel like part of his family. Sliding my arm around Juanna's plump waist we walked together with Ulpiano towards Alejandro's house for a celebratory merienda. The year's work completed, each one of us were smiling. Even Manuella. Catching the mood, Anthony and Miles skipped ahead beside her each waving a hay fork. Arms about each other's shoulders, I half expected Ed, Alejandro and Ignacio to break into a dance.

I turned back for a last look at quickly emptying Era. But for the thock of a football and cries of playing children, the threshing field would sleep till spring.

14

HARVEST FESTIVAL

For weeks Alejandro talked of nothing else. Now, here it was, the end of August and work over for the year.

"*Fiestas a mi casa,*" he'd say looking heavenwards and patting his tummy reminding me of his invitation.

For the hundredth time I forced a smile and nodded. *As if I could forget,* I thought ungraciously.

An immediate image of pyramids of Coxes and green Granny Smith apples came to me, and enormous yellow vegetable marrows balanced on end below the altar rail of our local church. And offerings of plaited loaves and crusty country bread piled on the crisp white altar cloth beside golden sheaves of corn shimmering in the slanting light filtering from the windows. The whole church reeked with the scent of ripening.

All is safely gathered in, oh thank the Lord, oh, thank the Lord, the harvest hymn circled my brain.

I saw nothing like that in Ruesga, for each family celebrated in their homes their own way and on days of their own choosing.

Dressed in our Sunday best, Ed and I joined Alejandro at the Juanon the following Sunday sometime after noon, and found him standing in the far corner by the one window, unusually shaved and scrubbed looking almost handsome in his clean checked shirt. I noticed he wore the same dirt encrusted canvas shoes he always wore. Ed ordered him a *clarete* and another for Ignacio, who at that moment stepped through the door. No sign of his brother-in-law Mariano nor his cousin Ulpiano, and I wondered where they were. Ed ordered some tortilla tapas, green olives, and a variety of pinchas to snack on. After standing for at least an hour and I was getting fidgety. Before we eat too much, better see what's going on in

"*Vamanos al otro Bar de Maria.*" Alejandro's suggestion took me off guard.

"What Maria's?" I exclaimed. "I thought you never darkened the upper bar's cursed Catholic doors."

"*Pero hoy es differente. Fiesta,*" he shrugged.

From the number of families we passed on the five-minute stroll to Maria's, not only our group, but the whole village seemed to be on the move.

"Looks crammed," I hesitated seeing the crush of people outside.

"*Feliz fiestas. Que dia mas bueno,*" As if we were regulars, Maria beamed welcoming Ed and me, ruffling Anthony's and Miles' hair at the same time. "*Clarete? Toma la mesa fuera.*"

Without even a glance towards Alejandro and Ignacio, she returned almost immediately with three saucers of appetizing *pinchas*; mussels-on-the shell drizzled with a spicy tomato sauce another of chopped kidney swimming in garlic gravy delicately garnished with chives and parsley, and one bearing translucent slivers of smoked horse meat.

I sank onto a shady bench under a ramada of dried branches and looked around at the crowded tables I'd envied so often walking by. Not wanting to with by even entering the establishment, Ed always refused. "It would be disloyal," he said. "Alejandro, and half the village want nothing to do with the Upper Bar because, not only are Maria's family Catholic, but they're Franco supporters, and it would be disloyal to my friends to drink with them."

"Wouldn't bother me," I remarked to Ed. "It's way more comfortable being able to sit."

"*Situo por uno mas?*" Ulpiano popped suddenly into view beside our table. All dressed up in a moon-white shirt, he looked shyly uncomfortable.

"*Juanna no es contigo?*" I asked, looking to see if she was behind him.

"*Juanna's esta a casa, ayudando.*" Ulpiano explained.

Leaning back in the shade, I looked around not bothering to make sense of their Spanish. Ed would speak enough for both of us.

"*Aurora. Mas vino. Mesa quatro.*" Shouting to her daughter, Maria's portly frame tottered by loaded with a pitcher of wine and tower of sparkling glasses. "*...y los dos,*" she barked at her teenage sons, "*Prisa. Limpio estos*"

From their lightening reaction, those boys dare not disobey their mother. Not so her husband. Nothing spurred him to move faster, neither the crush of clients, fiesta craziness, or his wife's orders. Infuriating to watch though he was, I secretly admired his calm in the midst of such mayhem. His expression stayed the same and I never saw him smile.

From the sun, it must have been after three by the time Manuella strolled up to where we were sitting to call us to eat.

"*Listo. Ven. Tiempo por comida.*" She stood by the table, her face dour, arms folded prepared to wait for as long it took to gather us up,

Never once had we been invited upstairs to the family's living quarters. We'd always sat round a table set up in the cool arched entry hall downstairs, or on a log outside in the *quadro*. Talking a little too loudly, we crowded the hall shushing and doing our best to compose ourselves to suit the occasion.

La Madre hovered at the top of the stairs dressed overall in her usual widow's black reminding me of a mother blackbird. Perhaps in concession to the special day, the plaited coils of her silver hair remained for once uncovered, and she had on a crisply ironed apron.

"*Bienvenidos. Adelante. Ven arriba. Ven, ven,*" she chirped, her beady eyes twinkling.

Taking both her hands, I bent forward, dutifully kissed both cheeks. So tiny her stature, the top of her head barely reached my chin.

"*Holà mi amiga.* There you are Juanna," I walked up behind her to see what she was frantically stirring in the casserole steaming on the open range. "Hmm. *Huele bien. Hace mucho calor, no?*"

"Anything I can do?" I offered feebly knowing she'd refuse.

"*Solamente sienta-te.*" She flustered, waving a wooden spoon. "I'll be with you pronto."

The room temperature was almost unbearable after the outside air and I quickly backed away and joined Anthony and Miles on the far side of the long table beside the one and only window.

"Air. Give me air," I sank beside them on a wooden bench fanning the faint trickle of air from the open window onto my face.

With the family occupied and focused on cooking, and the men cluster together shouting full volume, I had time to stare around without being thought rude.

An assortment of blackened iron pots, faded bunches of herbs, and smoked jamon suspended above the stove. Smoke-yellowed walls and oak beams, darkened what little light there was. The only functional "living room," clearly the kitchen was where the family sat, relaxed and cooked. Somehow, I had expected the living quarters to be more comfortable. One upholstered chair at least, an antique oak dresser, perhaps a display of decorative plates, and a comfortable rocking chair drawn close to the open hearth. Instead, a solitary wooden chest on the landing appeared to be the only furniture other than the kitchen table and chairs. Hardly decorative, a varnished and sticky fly-spotted paper swung from a beam and on the wall below hung an outdated give-away calendar depicting a snorting bull advertising THE BEST, TEN-YEAR AGED OSORNO BRANDY.

"That must be your mother and father's wedding photo, no?" I asked La Madre switching my attention to the sepia photo of a stiff unsmiling couple on the wall. "Alejandro takes after you, Señora, and

I can see Manuella's and Ignacio's likeness in their father."

Piercing, their eyes stared stonily into the room, and I shifted uneasily wondering if they disapproved of all this carousing in their home.

Looking past them through the pair of glass French doors leading directly off the kitchen, I could just make out two cell-like, windowless rooms each with a solitary Matrimonio brass bed over which hung a lone crucifix. They share beds, I realized taken aback. Two grown brothers in one bed, and Madre and Manuella in the other till she married and moved in with Mariano. I pictured the frail form of La Madre lying alone and falling to sleep by the flickering light from the fire's dying embers.

Though Juanna and Manuella prepared the food and did most of the cooking, La Madre reigned queen of her kitchen. Patiently lifting and closing pot-lids they allowed La Madre the honor of correcting the seasonings. I found their kindness touching to watch. Their respectful deferment towards the old lady.

"*Eh, Isabel, aqui. Todo buena?*" Ulpiano waved his hand and got my attention.

"Here Juanna. Come sit by me," I patted the space beside me.

"*Momento,*" she puffed placing a plate of tapas on the table.

I kept my hands on my lap hesitant to spoil such a beautifully set table by touching a thing. Sparkling glassware, ominous numbers of plates, paper napkins and hunks of bread at every place, a large oval serving plate of raw slices of tomato and onion interspersed with spears of tinned white asparagus swimming in olive oil took pride of place in the center.

"*Ahora,*" La Madre nodded before taking her place at the head of the table between Ignacio and Alejandro.

Neither household owned more than three or four chairs, but somehow, they'd rustled up enough to seat all ten of us. And the banquet table, how did they come by that? Peeking under its festive, yellow flowery cloth I saw it was actually two small tables pushed together.

Chairs scraping, the five men settled round the table, then almost immediately, Ignacio pushed back.

"*Bienvenidos. Feliz fiestas.*" He toasted looking in turn at each one of us.

"*Feliz fiestas.*" The kitchen exploded into happy clapping and raising of glasses.

"*Salude, pesetas y tiempo de costar los,*" we chorused. "Health, money and time to enjoy them."

Shy as always, Mariano fixed his eyes on his wife's and repeated the toast.

"*Que tonto,*" Manuella nudged him coyly.

"*Un comida por los millonarios,*" I declared in Spanish, admiringly.

"*Vino. Vino, fresca,* cool wine," frequently disappearing downstairs to refill the earthenware jug of wine in the bodega, Ignacio made sure every glass stayed filled.

A steaming soup dish of cockles, and prawns sprinkled heavily with parsley appeared on the table for Ulpiano to ladle out. But for a pile of sucked clean shells every bowl soon emptied.

Next came course number three; a garlic-flavored potato and chicken dish which included its liver, neck and heart garnished with scarlet runner beans.

"*Guarda los tenedores,*" Manuella instructed waving a fork before handing back out our rinsed plates.

"*Y ahora, le major de toda. Coño picante. Tienne tres guindas enteros.*" Ulpiano wiggled his pinkie and jabbed the chile lewdly laughing at his private joke saying, "*Juanna gusta un un pica a veces.*"

"Hmm. *Delicioso,*" I sniffed ignoring the insinuation.

Her round cheeks flushed, his beloved Juanna set down a heavy enamel dish, and lifting the lid smiled as we broke out clapping.

Gruesome sounds of sucking silenced our chatter as marrow, meat, cartilage, juices, tiny morsels were stripped from every bone. I watched Manuella amazed as she drew a clutch of rabbit ribs through her teeth. I had to look away when I saw Alejandro sink his teeth into a rabbit's skull and probe every nook and cranny with his tongue. Even La Madre ate with her fingers. No point being ladylike, with an exaggerated wink I picked up a bone, nibbled a rabbit face with my front teeth and set my sons giggling.

When at last the plates gleamed licked and clean, Manuella let out a contented goat-like belch.

"*Bien dia por las cabras,*" we chorused as she stood to gather our plates.

We sat back grateful for the break before dessert. Perfect timing, I looked around for the bathroom.

"*Quiero cuarto de bano. Donde es?*" I asked not seeing one.

Instead of pointing, Manuella and Juanna exchanged glances.

"*Ven con migo,*" Manuella headed down the stairs and pointed into the cow stalls and at the squares of newspaper hanging from a wire.

"*Ojo.*" She said tapping a finger to her eye showing me she'd keep a lookout. Manuella turned her back but stayed where she was. A little unnerved I cautiously lifted my skirt. As I let go all eight cows shifted uneasily, stared at me with their big brown eyes and peed.

By the time we returned, the dirty plates were gone, breadcrumbs swept, the table re-laid with liqueur and champagne glasses, a set of espresso coffee cups, and a set of scalloped glass plates.

"*Champagne,*" Ignacio exclaimed as the cork flew over the table with a fizzle and we covered our ears pretending the pop louder than it was.

"*Olé. Bravo.*" The children joined us in the round of clapping and clink of glasses.

"*La vida de millonarios,*" Ed complimented Alejandro for the extravagent meal, clapping him on the back. "*Reyes et Rienas.*"

One could almost see Alejandro's chest puff. He never tired of the compliment and smiled proudly each time. It was true, he did live the life of the wealthy in the sense he owned land, two large homes, wanted for nothing and time was his own.

"*Cafe? Torta?*" Juanna hovered over the table, a heavily iced slice of sponge poised on her knife.

"*No puedo. No puedo.* Not another morsel," I patted my belly, though I might as well have kept my mouth shut, for she tipped a large slice on my plate ignoring at my protestations. Not La Madre and our hosts, they fell on their cake as if they hadn't eaten for a week. I couldn't believe how much they relished what to me was a rather boring vanilla sponge. But Mercedes was right. She insisted *Torte* was a treat, the perfect gift when I asked what I should take to their fiesta. Unable to speak for the cake in her mouth, I watched Manuella in awe as she thrust out her plate for a second helping even while cramming the last of the cake crumbs into her mouth.

Relaxed and replete after such a great feast, we settled round the table to laugh and talk while the men puffed smoke rings from fat cigars, and swilled their brandy. Well away, Ulpiano stood up and unbuttoning his shirt stripped to his undervest. Snapping his fingers and stamping his feet his face became dreamy as the first notes of *"Una paloma blanca...."* fell into the room.

"Canta no llores...Besame..." He sang "don't cry, kiss me." His eyes misted with sadness and I thought he might cry.

"Bastante. Silencio. Cuidado malo," Juanna pulled at his shirttails and forced him back onto his chair. "Enough, bad boy!" She warned, waving her knife threateningly at her husband.

"We should get going if we're to rest a little before the evening's *Baille.*" I rose from the table to leave before the fiesta disintegrated into a fight.

Dusk already softening grey stone of Ruesga's hard edges by the time we stumbled outside, Ruesga shimmered in a wash of Prussian blue. I stopped in the quiet of the lane to gaze at the Evening Star dangling over the Almonga's silhouette.

Let this summer to be as unending as your light, I whispered.

Overcome by one of those rare moments of such happiness, a shudder ran through my body.

"Well, that was some meal," Ed remarked. "Do you imagine they always put on such a feast to celebrate the end of harvest?"

They did. Invited every year, we took part in the tradition.

15

WHAT DO YOU DO?

"What do you do all that time staying year after year in a village that doesn't even have a shop?" a friend questioned over the phone.

"Do?" I bridled picturing the blissful summers we spent every year in Ruesga.

"Same as you," I snapped. "Get up. Dress. Eat, do chores, work and sleep."

"We don't even have time to read we're so busy... living," I emphasized the word living knowing she had no idea what I meant.

Crouched on the bottom stair by the telephone table, I stretched the cable as far as it allowed and held the receiver away from my ear, and...my kids...did I tell you... my friend prattled on.

The only difference from your day, I wanted to retort, is everything in my day happens naturally at a pace all its own, not dictated by timetables or a boss in some stuffy office. I didn't elaborate.

From what you tell me, the village hasn't even boast a shop, so what about food?

"No problemo. Bread arrives twice a day from the neighboring town and the chicken truck delivers twice a week." I refrained from adding, fully feathered and alive, and that unable to bear their pathetic squawking, I paid extra to buy one plucked, gutted, and ready for the pot.

Shattering Ruesga's peace, from at least half a mile away the screeched megaphone announcements began. Pollo, pollo. Pan, pan. Each driver called the housewives from their houses. I dropped whatever I was doing and rushed to join the untidy line outside the Juanon. Listening in on their gossip was the perfect opportunity for me to work on my Spanish and untangle their incomprehensible chatter.

Definitely not England, my visits to the butcher in Cervera, meant at least an hour's wait in line twice a week. With no refrigerator or ice to preserve food for more than a day, I had no choice. Jammed between half a gaggle of massively-thighed and bosomed ladies in a space more suitable for four people at most, I took in the theatrical scene.

A woman with arms as brawny as a boxer's, a glinting cleaver gripped in her hand appeared through the beaded curtain behind the counter with a flourish, a bloodied apron tied over her clothes. Expressionless, she surveyed her audience, summoned the first customer forward, not to take her order it seemed, but to extract and exchange news. The waiting crowd fell silent hopeful a morsel of gossip let slip. Finally, she disappeared behind the bead curtain with the customer's order penciled on a scrap of paper, to unhurriedly reappear and slap each item on the counter.

Uno kilo de puerco, dos kilos de tenera, seis rognones, una dozena chorizos salchicas, lomo... each customer's list of cuts unfurled endlessly. I calculated the time. Five women ahead of me. Another hour at least. Patient as the waiting women around me, I relaxed.

"How do you entertain your boys in such a tiny village?" My friend's irritating voice pierced my reverie.

"Entertain?" I scoffed. "Never see them. Except to eat and sleep, they're off all day long doing whatever kids do. One of the reasons we go there is because it's safe for them to run wild…"

"Parcel." The postman's voice called me to open the door. Bang. Bang. The doorknocker hammered twice as his outline blocked the frosted glass panels.

"Sorry…have to go. It's the postman." Thankful, I rolled my eyes and cut off my friend.

Reeling from a blast of icy air I slammed the front door shut impatient to scrabble at the knotted string. Ripping away the outer layer, a scrap of paper fluttered to the floor.

ISABEL "oregano de Lores. Brazos. Besos. Juanna y Ulpiano," I deciphered the scrawled uneven mix of penciled capital and cursive lettering. I pictured Juanna peering over Ulpiano's shoulder chivvying him on as he struggled to form the letters of each word.

Inside, I found a bundle of dried oregano sprigs of purple flowers and leaves wrapped in newspaper and tied with rough twine. Smoothing the crumpled newsprint, I read the date aloud. 17th Agosto 1976. Clutching the bundle against my sweater, I inhaled its heady scent and was immediately back in the mountains above the tiny village of Lores with Ulpiano and Juanna gathering the pungent herb beneath a cloudless sky.

"Thank you. I miss you too," I whispered, touching the message to my lips. So much more than those simple words, their scrawled note declared their love.

"What perfect timing." I wanted to cry.

Images of afternoon merienda in the high fields with our Spanish family flashed in my mind, then creaking homeward behind a loaded cart with Anthony and Miles peering from the top half buried by stalks of golden grain. A deep ache that I knew would not leave me till summer engulfed me. Three o'clock, day light already melting into night. How could I not yearn to be back in Spain far from England's gloomy, damp, grey, January.

What did I do all day, indeed, I muttered. *Damn nuisance,* I cursed unable to get the hint of disapproval in my friend's question out of my head.

Wednesday, my one day off from work. The boys at school, Ed

at his college, I had the house to myself. I missed the freedom of the seaside home where Anthony and Miles had lived since they were born. Not my choice, I'd been forced to sell. Do my duty for Anthony's sake. His need for special schooling. So, when an opportunity to share free private tuition in London with the two deaf daughters of a woman I'd met, I jumped at the chance, sold my flat and moved.

Suddenly depressed, all morning defensive answers made me more and more miserable. The sacrifice paid off, I convinced myself. Anthony can fit into both the deaf and hearing world, and even knows a little Spanish.

But still, I worried, City living with no place for my boys to run and play unsupervised except our back garden, and when I took them to the park. was no way to develop, None the better for venting, I made a face. Timetables, deadlines, routines were not for me. I closed my eyes unable to see a way out.

And Ed as their step-dad? Hardly an okay role model with his drunken rages after evenings spent in the pub, before swaying through the front door, his eyes scarily narrowed from the anger pent inside him.

Ed's and my lives ran on parallel tracks. His work days traveling three hours by train to lecture at Portsmouth University, and his free time bashing a golf ball from hole to hole, that is when he wasn't downing beers and playing darts at the pub with his mates. Not the family experience I wanted for my children.

Loud bleeping signaled the end of the wash cycle telling me to unload. I threw the heavy sheets into the tumble dryer triggering a flashback of laundry day in Ruesga bent over Mercedes' bath tub up to my elbows in cold water like the village women kneeling at the river's edge below the bridge. Strolling back to our tent the basin of washing balanced on my hip, I often found myself humming. *It's a beautiful day today and whatever I've got to do, it's a beautiful day for doing it that's true…,* The songs words rang. Not like a chore at all, I draped every bush I could find with dripping wash transforming the meadow to a colorful composition.

Clonk, with a final whirr, the spin-drier shook to a stop and brought me back to the grey of England. With each garment, each sheet and towel pulled from the tumble drier, I unfurled another memory. Transported back, I could almost feel the cool long grass brush my ankles as I spread the sheets on the ground as Mercedes instructed. Lay the sheets flat in the field to dry. *The greener the grass, the whiter the wash.*

A howl of wind rattled the front door reminding me winter raged outside. The sound made me shiver despite central heating and I buttoned my cardigan up to my neck. Poor Alejandro and La Madre in their unheated house I thought. Alejandro had blown on his fingers describing how he passed the winter.

"Tierra 'elado, Entoces no puedo hacer nada fuera pero cuidar mes vacas y animales, corta leña por el fuego, hacer cestos y dormito junto al fuego comiendo, bebiendo, engordiendo como un bicho hinchado," he laughed, and bulging his cheeks to imitate a fat, bloated bug.

I pictured his sun-browned skin faded, pasty-white, sluggish, Alejandro holed up in the semi-dark of his kitchen weaving baskets by the light of a hurricane lamp. It was hard to imagine how a man of the earth like him with his large sausage fingers could weave the supple lengths of willow to such perfection. An image came to me. Alejandro huddled on a stool upstairs above the cowshed before the open hearth, beside his dozing mother, reaching for a twig of willow from the pile beside him. The soft breathing of La Madre, the fire's spit and crackle, the swish of willow, the only sounds.

I turned to look at my treasures on the kitchen window sill; the three baskets made by Alejandro. No bigger than a robin's nest, gruffly thrust the tiniest, most beautifully crafted basket I'd ever seen into my hand. Beside them lay the fragment of threshing sledge I found abandoned in the uncut grass ringing *la Era* six years back. Cradling the oak scrap in my palm, I rubbed its polished surface against my cheek, and heard again the sigh of wood sliding over grain and the gentle hiss of sickle and scythe slicing air.

I pulled the dried load into the laundry basket. Began folding… the expanse of green threshing floor spread below me as if I were leaning over the dam wall as I liked to do after my regular morning swim, gazing down at *la Era* where it lay quietly empty, holding its breath, as if in waiting for the villagers to set it in motion again. The sun warm on my back, checking, re-checking, I fixed every golden *corona*, yellow monton of grain, threshing sledge and plodding cow in my mind fearful of the day the ancient scene I witnessed would be no more than a memory.

Aren't you ever bored? Aren't you ever bored? My friends question still buzzed.

"Stupid bitch. Couldn't she see our days were filled?" I swatted my friend's question to the wall and returned to my remembering.

If we weren't helping our adopted family in the fields, or cooking meals on the open fire outside our tents, we were exploring distant villages, clambering the hills to reach a wildflower meadow, or picnicking beneath a cloudless sky.

And then, fiestas, Bull Fights, the traveling circus that trundled into town. Hardly a week passed without a celebration in some village close by. Saint's Days, National Holidays, Cervera's Fiesta of the Waiters, the Dianna, Ruesga's street fiesta drinking sweet wine in every house, the annual Cow Fair on a steep hillside just over the mountain pass, the Sardine festival that filled the open field outside Cervera with a stomach-turning smell of frying. Picking wild herbs, oregano from the mountain crags with Ulpiano and Juanna. Memories crowded my mind.

Time to pick the boys up from their schools. I bundled up and headed into the biting cold. Ed wouldn't be back till late, after his darts match was over, and not till the pub pushed him and his pals onto the street. Good, an evening with just my boys free to cuddle and act as silly as we chose.

16

JUANNA'S BIRTHPLACE

Our routine changed with harvest over. We spent more time up at the lake, and going on little adventures to places we'd never got around to seeing like Trillo at the head of the valley to hike along to river to the cow-shaped mountain of Curavaca. Now we knew eachother better, Juanna turned up at our tent home quite often just to watch me work at whatever I was doing, which that day, was energetically scouring the inside of my main cooking pot with wood ash from our fire.

"Holá Juanna. I've been wanting to ask you something," I greeted her as she strolled into the meadow.

I wiped the black from my hands on the grass and perched on the log beside her.

"How would you like to go on a couple of day trips with us one of these days? Maybe this weekend even. Anyplace you and Ulpiano especially want to visit?"

"My home. The house where I was born," she blurted spontaneously. "It's near the National Park of Fuente De. Oh, I'd love to see my sister again in case...." her sentence hung unfinished. Wistful, her voice softened, "It's been so long...fifteen years now. She and her husband moved in after our parents died, after Ulpiano and I were married and moved to Ruesga. I've not been back since. Ulpiano's off work the whole weekend."

"Saturday then?" We set the day.

Ours would be their first long car ride, she told me. So used to taking cars for granted, I'd never thought much of what it would mean to someone who'd never traveled in one. When I thought about it, the only vehicle I'd seen in the village apart from our own beat-up mini, was the twice daily bread van.

I knew she and Ulpiano had taken a couple of train rides to Santander's coast to see his niece, Pilli, Ulpiano's only other surviving relative apart from his brother, Mariano, but other than that and a couple of bus trips, they rarely ventured from home. Except the daily trip to work when Ulpiano traveled in an open lorry to and from the coalmine where he spent ten hours working in a flooded mineshaft.

Early Saturday, Ed and I found Juanna and Ulpiano stiff and solemn ready waiting on their front step formally dressed in their best clothes. Too big an adventure to be their bubbly selves, they greeted us with a tight smile before clambering silently into the back seat. They spoke little except to occasionally call out names of places they recognized.

"*Hay Lores. Miré.*" Ulpiano pointed excitedly through the window. "On that slope over there below those rocks is where we find purple oregano about this time of year. It's a full day's hike from Ruesga, but if you'd like to come, we're planning on going next week."

I looked back at the disappearing jumble of red rooves clustered at the base of the mountains as we ground slowly round the bend toward the pass of Piedras Luengas where Ed and I always liked to stop. He pulled the mini onto the grass verge. Jumping from the cramped mini, I spread my arms like wings, and leaned into the westerly sea wind gulping mouthfuls of air. Standing with one foot in the Province of Santander, and one in Palencia, the view from the Divide stunned me to silence every time.

Turning, I scanned the open pasture beyond the scrub oak forest to my left tracking a flock of white specks moving across the mountain meadow we'd hiked the year before. And a memory flooded back of the idyllic day we'd come across a shepherd and sat awhile with him in the silent landscape carpeted with yellow crocus and purple clover. Before we left him, the shepherd pointed out a ground spring to the boys, and I remembered how he shook his head seeing our modern leather water bottles lined with plastic and showed us his better insulated, pitch-lined bottle covered with curly white sheep's wool.

"*Miré...Aguilas.* Look two pairs of Eagles," Ulpiano exclaimed, spotting four faint dots slowly circling below the overlook where we stood.

Their plaintive calls floated from the sky though I couldn't make them out at first, not until they swooped up and over our heads on an updraft invisible to me. I followed them sailing towards the mountain crest and vanish like two kites cut loose from their strings.

"Our first summer we had a picnic up there, Juanna." I pointed, laughing at the memory. "Well, the goats had a picnic. They ate most of it, cloth and all. Can you imagine, while we hiked up to those rocks, we left food spread out on a tablecloth. No wonder a small herd of goats came and ate everything in sight, even Miles' sweater. They actually stayed standing on our picnic cloth staring as if we were crazed, and refusing to budge even when we ran at them yelling. The only one scared was Miles. He burst into tears thinking we were upset, poor boy. He was only four, then. Eventually we managed to shoo them away and got him to see the funny side and laugh."

"Hey chatterboxes, better get a move on," Ed summoned us to the car.

Crossing the pass, we almost immediately dropped into the sunless gloom of a thickly wooded forest of giant silver-barked beech trees whose branches spread so wide and tall they formed a canopy over our heads. Not one of us spoke till the forest ended and we entered the sunlight of the open road and Santander's rich farmland unfurled before us twenty miles below.

"We're getting close. I can smell we are." Juanna sat bolt upright chattering excitedly as she sensed we neared her childhood home, pointing first one way, then the other as we passed places she recognized.

"Oh look, Ulpiano, that house in that orchard across the river, isn't that my girlfriend's house where I used to stay?" She wound down the window and looked back at a stone farmhouse nestled in the hamlet across the river.

"We can stop there first and see if she's still lives there if you like before going to your old home," I told her.

"No. No. I must see my sister first," she shook her head.

Juanna pulled herself forward, leaned over the passenger seat with her chin almost touching my shoulder, and tapped me frantically.

"Go slow. Now. Now, turn. Here. Here," Juanna shouted pointing out an overgrown lane Ed had already dismissed as impassable. Swerving left Ed nosed the mini onto the bumpy track. But after no more than a hundred yards, the searing grind of undercarriage scraping earth forced him to brake to a halt.

"Out, everyone. That's it. We'll leave the car parked here." Ed leaped from the driver's seat to examine the damage.

"From here we have to climb the rest of the way on foot anyway. It's a bit of a slog and will take about an hour to get there." Juanna pushed her door open impatient to get started.

A rough, little used lane barely wide enough for a cart disappeared into a shady arc of Chestnut and Beech. Muffled by the soft carpet of rotting leaves, not a footfall, not a rustle could be heard as, the four of us trod one behind the other through stepping stones of light and shadow scattered beneath the trees.

Rounding a corner, we startled a family of javeline, rooting for nuts, I wasn't sure if we, or they, were surprised the most. We froze. The brown and white striped sow and her five piglets fled squealing into the deep shadows.

Plod. Plod. One foot before the other, the mountain climb

seemed unending. Stubby grass and fallen leaves gave way to sun-baked earth and stone once we emerged into the open above the treeline.

Pausing beside a spring to catch our breath, I gratefully took my turn to gulp its icy water seeping from a moss-covered mound, and splash my reddened face.

"Wow. Look how far we've already climbed. And to think you walked from here everyday to get to school, Juanna." I waved my hand towards the valley tucked out of sight below Fuente Dé's National Park.

"Not too long now, just around the next corner," Ulpiano put his arm around Juanna's shoulders. "Well, are you ready to see your sister?"

Nodding, Juanna ran her hand through her curls and tucked in her blouse and smooth her skirt. Her face crumpled as if she might break down in tears.

Rounding the final bend as we approached the house, no cry of welcome, but an agonized scream stopped us dead in our tracks. Catching sight of us from an upper balcony festooned with strands of sheep's wool she'd been beating, a woman threw down her stick with a cry and disappeared.

Bursting from the lower level, the woman ran with arms outstretched calling "*Hermana. Hermana,* Sister. Sister," and flung herself at Juanna.

"Who's died? What's happened sister? Are you ill?" She sobbed, for nobody, but nobody made the arduous vertical climb unless to tell of some dreadful tragedy or death. Seeing us, she assumed the worst.

Josephina gripped Juanna's face between her hands and stared deep into her sister's eyes probing for the truth.

Through all the tears, for by then Juanna and Ulpiano were weeping too, it took a little time to convince Josephina all was well. Now from joy, half laughing, half crying, clamping Juanna's arm under her own, Josephina propelled her towards the kitchen.

"*Sentarse. Sentarse.* Sit," she waved towards the hand-hewn oak table. "*Soy Josephina. Bienvenidos. Tengo grand illusion de conocerte.* I'm pleased to meet my sister's friends."

Chattering all the while, Josephina set four glasses on the table and filled them with wine. From the occasional word I could pick out, I gathered she expected us to stay for Comida, that it wouldn't take her long to light the oven, make bread and prepare the meal. We weren't expecting company...excuse my clothes." Josephina smiled apologetically dusting down her apron.

Grabbing a handful of broom she snapped the dry twigs in two, propped them in the open fireplace of the iron range soon had a blazing fire going. She made it look so easy, I thought admiringly. Then I noticed the range. Ingenious. It's open fire not only heated a pot on a trivet, two ovens, and two iron top plates, but a brick bread oven set in the chimneybreast behind a quaint arched door. And, as I was surprised to see water as well in copper tank built along one side.

Hurrying back to the table Josephina dragged her chair close, clasped Juanna's hands between hers, kissing and pressing them to her heart as if fearing her sister would vanish. Talking and laughing at top speed, their words tumbled so fast, I made out only a tenth of what they were saying.

"My heart stopped when I saw you. I assumed you must be dying or suffered some dreadful disease," Josephina repeated over and over continuously leaning forward to pinch Juanna's cheeks to convince herself she was fine. "I was so worried, sister. *No me creo! Que tu es aqui con migo.*" I can't believe you're really here with me. *Ayee, que feliz estoy.* Oh, how happy I am to see you," she cooed. "We never get visitors you see," she added turning to us.

Delighting in their open joy at being together, I smiled. No mistaking they were sisters. I looked from one to the other. Same stocky figure, same dark curly hair, same gestures, and the full-throated way they threw back their heads when they laughed.

"My husband and three boys, (yes sister, I have three grown sons now,) are up the mountain but will be back in a couple of hours," she explained to us before turning again to Juanna.

Engrossed in swapping family news, the rest of us might as well have been invisible. Ulpiano tactfully pushed back his chair, and stood up.

"Come. Let's leave the two of them to catch up. I know the place pretty well and can show you around while we wait for them." He headed towards the door.

After the chill of the stone kitchen, it felt good to be out in the sunshine. A cluster of perhaps five buildings ringed a wide terrace of land carved from the mountain, though I could see their home comprised the only human dwelling. Enormous by Ruesga's standards, the two-foot-thick granite structure three floors high, teetered perilously on the steep mountainside above the valley. The balcony along two sides of the upper floor was a surprise for none existed in our village. In Ruesga windowless walls lined the lanes and houses faced inwards onto a *quadro* for protection from the wind and privacy. As expected, the ground level cow byre below the living quarters held nothing but the sweet aroma of hay-scented patties.

Cows in upper pasture," Ulpiano explained.

Still curious about the strands of sheep's wool I'd seen Josephine beating when we arrived, I opened my mouth about to ask.

"That's the matted wool from a sheep's underbelly left over from shearing. It's no good for weaving so we use it to stuff our mattresses. Great to sleep on don't you agree?" Ulpiano answered my unspoken question. "The knots and lumps need to be beaten out and aired in the sun two or three times a year."

The empty *quadro* glowed with sunshine. A calming sound of running water spilled from the spring-fed trough. A harem of hens pecked the manure heap guarded by the largest rooster imaginable. As we neared, the magnificent bird drew himself full height, flapped his wings and crowing his ownership, warned us to keep well away. One look from his beady eye and display of his murderous talons was enough for me. I knew from a scary experience with Alejandro's rooster who'd once gone for the worm-like veins in my ankles, to keep my distance.

A mongrel mix I didn't quite like the look of, slunk from the shadows tailing us and glaring suspiciously as we opened and shut doors of each building.

"We'll begin with the shearing shed," Ulpiano, our leader, announced, but one look, and the pungent smell of dried sheep droppings drove us quickly back outside.

The hay loft and sweet-scented hay, the smoke house with its four hanging hams, strings of chorizo and mysterious sausages, the storage sheds of hand carved ploughs, rakes and farm tools, we admired everything on our tour.

"Oh, there you are my beauties," I said stopping in front of the pigsty.

"*Here piggy-wiggies. Dance piggy-wiggies,*" I crooned, throwing them a couple of tufts of chickweed I spotted growing outside their pen to set them dancing. There's just something about them I've always loved. The sound of their snorting and their four-footed dance when they were excited. I could have stayed playing with them for hours but Ulpiano moved us on.

"I want to see how their rabbits are doing," Ulpiano swung open the door to the dimly lit shed flooding it with sudden light and set them scampering. "Look at the size of those rabbits. Must be fifty at least." He stared excitedly and let out a sigh before dragging us away.

Leaving the *quadro*, Ulpiano waved his stick upward and set off ahead of us up the mountain to a wire-enclosed vegetable patch carved into the hillside bordered mysteriously along the outer fence by a single row of flaming red gladioli. Why gladioli? I forgot to ask. Rows of healthy vegetables burst from the furrows; beans, carrots, onions, garlic, potatoes, canes of tomatoes among many others. Just stuck there on the mountain side above the house seemed a peculiar place to grow vegetables, but clearly it worked. We stood a few moments to watch a heavily laden honeybee crash-land a scarlet blossom of a runner bean and then buzz past us to the hives I could see grouped above us on the purple vetch and clover covered the hillside. And as we climbed towards them I became aware the air hummed thick with bees.

The sun, hot but not too fierce felt warm on my skin. I was ready to stop when Ulpiano called a halt. I turned to gaze at the breathtaking view; the snaking line of green way below me in the valley where we'd abandoned the car; the softly rounded mountain range so different to the grey jagged peaks surrounding Ruesga.

"That's Fuente Dé National Park where the road ends" Ulpiano pointed left. "Sadly, many tourists, many hikers. People like this." Shaking his head, Ulpiano bunched his fingers indicating the crush of people.

"Coming?" He waved his stout walking stick towards the crest, his mind set on meeting up with the men and picking purple oregano and *tè* in the higher rocky outcrops.

"I'll come." Ed jumped to his feet eager for action.

"Not me. I'm happy staying put." I shook my head.

Alone at last on the mountainside with nobody to interrupt my thoughts, I unbuttoned my blouse, wriggled a place to settle in the long stems of meadow grass. Drowsy from a combination of laziness and high altitude, I flopped backwards and stared into the giddying blue till my eyes flickered shut. Barely had they closed, when voices infiltrated my consciousness. Buttoning my blouse, I sprung to my feet just as our host's three sons bounded into view leading a donkey half buried by the load of hay each carried on its back.

Nearing, the three boys stood awkwardly in front of me unsure whether to acknowledge me or keep on moving.

"*Vienne pronto*," one of the older boys muttered shyly, pointing to the distant figures of a man I guessed to be Josephina's husband, and Ed and Ulpiano way above striding down the mountain towards us with that easy swing of country men in tune with the land.

Spanish style exchanging formal greetings. Shaking hands, bowing slightly, Ulpiano introduced me to Josephina's and Thomàs' sons.

Encantado. Pleased to meet you. *Mucho gusto.* My pleasure. *Encantado,* Isabel meet Thomàs. Isabel meet Simòn, and so on, we went through the ritual feeling a little foolish to be standing on a mountainside making such formal introductions.

Excusing themselves with a nod, the three boys chased on ahead with their donkeys whooping and yelling. Arriving back in the *quadro,* we found the boys at the trough splashing each other and mucking about when clearly they were supposed to be washing up for lunch. Seeing us, they fell quiet and headed to the kitchen looking a little shamefaced.

I don't recall details of the *comida* itself, only that it was delicious and a feast. Freshly picked salad of raw onion and tomato before the main meat dish of richly spiced rabbit casserole served with potatoes, and vegetables pulled from the garden, and slabs of crusty, newly-baked bread. Josephina and Juanna rustled up the magnificent meal in the space of a few hours, and even managed to whip up a dessert of custard flan made from her farm eggs and milk. Cool and fresh, wine poured from an earthenware jug flowed by the tumbler. So many toasts, I just had to refuse.

"You can always roll down the hillside," someone teased when I desisted.

As at the end of every celebration, the men leaned back in their chairs and puffed cigars over copas of brandy and sips of bitter solos, black coffee, while the two sisters fussed around clearing the table and washing dishes.

Forbidden to help, I stayed at the table wrapped in thought trying to imagine Josephina's life, and how it would be to live cut off from social interaction. Self-sufficiency was one thing, but if someone fell ill or the house caught fire, what then? No phone, no proper road, no way to get help but the race down the mountain, what a tough way to live.

I studied her matronly figure. Face flushed, sleeves rolled up, broad hands reddened from the piping hot water her middle son obediently carried for her from the stove, the no nonsense speed she scrubbed and soaped the dishes, her demeanor made it clear she was chief-in-charge, and those three strapping sons around the table were hers to command. I so wanted to sit with her and ask about her life. A dozen questions buzzed. But this wasn't the time and kept silent.

Simòn, the eldest son, excused himself and returned a few minutes later, spruced and immaculate in a crisp white shirt and hair slicked flat.

"He's courting," his dad explained in a hoarse stage whisper from behind his hand, unable to disguise his pride. "My son's taking his sweetheart to their first dance."

Where on earth… How did the poor boy manage to even find a date let alone get there.

"OK if I take Blackie? I'll be back to feed the animals in time tomorrow. Julio will do the milking for me." Simòn begged his dad to borrow a donkey like any adolescent from wanting his father's car.

We trooped outside partly to see him off and partly because the time had come for us to pile back into the car and make the long drive home.

Legs dangling, feet almost touching the ground, astride Blackie, son and donkey receded jauntily from sight. I pictured the romantic scene, the two shy lovers under the stars mounted on poor Blackie, she riding sidesaddle behind him with her arms clasped around his waist, head pressed to his back whispering in his ear.

On the drive back, too absorbed in reliving the day's reunion, I guessed, Ulpiano and Juanna spoke little.

No moon, but a million stars hung in the pitch night sky by the time we swung into Ruesga. A hurricane lamp blazed in Mercedes kitchen. Tucking into an oozing omelet, my boys looked up from the table smiling as I rushed to hug them.

"I missed you, darlings. Did you have a good time with Mercedes?"

17

ULPIANO AND JUANNA'S PICNIC

Perhaps in return for our trip together, Juanna and Ulpiano planned a surprise picnic for us. All I knew was we would walk to the next valley over with Juanna, while Ulpianno and *El Cazador*, the hunter friend of his, would set off at first light by a different route to set up the picnic site before we joined them.

"Tell. Tell us, where," we begged them.

"You'll see." They answered, waving vaguely towards our meeting place somewhere over the mountains.

"Buenas, Must have overslept," he mumbled and set off to pee by the river. Demanded coffee, eggs, bacon, toast and marmalade when he returned.

"Hey, in case you've forgotten, today is Ulpiano's picnic treat. Juanna should be here to collect us in an hour," I called after him.

Breakfast devoured, dishes washed and piled on their sides to dry, focused on scouring the last pan with ashes from the fire, when two stout legs appeared before me, and there she was, Juanna. Silent. Smiling, her plump arms, creased like rhizomes, sprouting from her flowered, sleeveless dress, she stood beside me in the meadow puffing gently from her two-mile walk from her home.

"*Holá. Buen dia, Juanna. Momento.*" Wiping my hands dry on the grass. I jumped to my feet, wrapped my arms about her and surrendered to one of her breath-emptying bear hugs.

"*No hay prisa,*" she said calmly, throwing her walking cane on the grass and flopping into one of our folding chairs.

I loved the woman. The unabashed bounce of her. No somber black or matronly aprons for that lady, her legs un-stockinged and exposed below the knee, her tight dark curls un-scarfed, Juanna flouted convention. Ignoring her peers, she laughed, told coarse jokes, sang full-throated *fabado* style, and set the red roof tiles rattling. She and Ulpiano flirted openly with each other and acted silly, and didn't care who saw and even ventured into the bar if I, a woman, was also there. Defiant, she'd stand beside me, arms crossed, uncharacteristically mute, stoically refusing all drinks except lemonade. Nobody was going to label her a loose woman or a drunk.

"*Buen dia por una comida del campo,*" Juanna said getting to her feet as a way of telling us we should get going.

I looked at her canvas slip-ons, and bare head, then at our sturdy *Cherookas* with their heavy rubber treads, thick socks, the long-sleeved shirts tied about our waists, and sunhats, fully kitted out with water bottle, fanny pack, binoculars, wishing I were brave enough to be like her and carry nothing.

"*Listos? Vamanos.* Let's go." Juanna, looked up at the sun and clapped her hands together for us to follow.

Once past Gusto's house, the last house in the village, we were on our way. Ahead the unknown. Excitement. Adventure. We could feel it. The sun's warm blush on my skin, and clean sweep of sky overhead promised a perfect day. And I broke into a run racing my boys up the steep track onto the reservoir's dam.

"This way," Juanna pointed left to a small footpath leading away from the lake. "See, the old copper mine? The pass to our picnic valley is just above."

I shaded my eyes squinting in the bright light and way in the distance near the top of the mountain, I made out a gaping mine shaft below the saddle. I'd often noticed the path from the lake and couldn't imagine why I'd not trekked it before.

Trudging one behind the other, I dropped back to be the last in line until sound faded and everything around me became mine: the sky, the cropped grass, purple vetch and clover, and scented wild thyme. The slope out of the valley steepened and we began to climb. The path disintegrated to scree making it difficult for my boots to find firm footholds. Slower now, Juanna pulled ahead, her stout legs pumping rhythmically.

The sun on my back burned though my shirt, my cheeks reddened and I ran my tongue along my upper lip savoring the salt-sweat. Using my hat, I fanned my face grateful for any breeze.

"*Caricoles. Caricoles.* Come on you snails," I heard Juanna mock, and looking up spotted her sitting below the cleavage of the pass, her back propped against a granite shepherd's hut.

Legs straight in front of her, she laughed at seeing us reduced to crawling the rocky slope on all fours.

"Phew," I gasped flopping on the sheep-cropped grass beside her. "That was some climb."

I lay back and rested in silence until my breathing slowed to normal. I could have fallen asleep and stayed for hours. I forced myself to sitting and reaching for the bota and took a swig directly from its nozzle filling my mouth with its cooling liquid inadvertently dribbling some down my chin. The others, even Miles and Anthony never spilt a drop even holding Ed's *bota* at arms-length above their heads. Seamlessly, they aimed the stream of dilute *vino* and gaseosa mix into their open mouths.

"*Todo bien, que non, eh Tonio?* Eh, Milo?" Juanna reached over, squeezed their sunburned thighs, pinched their cheeks and loudly kissed them in turn. Wriggling from her grasp they managed to escape and scampered off to explore the mine tailings and hunt for copper flecked rocks.

I glanced at Ed. Looking more peasant than language professor, with his long pants and rolled up sleeves, black felt *boina* angled over his left ear like his friends, then drew his *metcha* from his upper pocket and struck the flint with his free hand until the wick ignited. Inhaling deeply, he kept the roll-up dangling from his mouth like the village men. I wondered what he hoped to achieve with his desperate effort to blend in.

Contented to sit awhile, I traced the thin streak of blue of the reservoir along the valley below us. Beyond it, just visible, I made out the distant double humped peak of Curavaca crouched above the isolated village of Trillio like a cow the mountain was named for.

Revived, I stood up and followed Miles and Anthony to the stone-built refuge inside the corral. Delicious. Ten degrees cooler, my skin pimpled to goose-flesh.

"Over here, Mum, on the shepherd's bed."

Once my eyes adjusted, I made them stretched out under left-over scraps of dried-out heather and bracken on the stone built-in platform along the back wall.

"Not very comfy, but at least it's heated." I said poking my toe into the charred remnants in the open hearth beneath where a neat pile of twigs and squares of cut peat stood stacked ready beside it. "How would you like living here in this stone hut all summer with no-one to talk to but sheep?"

I knew I wouldn't last long huddled up there alone on the mountain with only the babble of sheep-talk, the howl of wind and spatter of rain to break the silence. I pictured Gusto's shepherd wrapped in his cloak curled asleep above the embers, the warm breath of his goats and sheep, the air, fetid, ankle-deep in droppings.

"Time to go," Juanna's silhouette filled the doorway. "Not long now to the top."

From the crest of the saddle, the slope eased gently into a high meadow softly green, quite unlike the arid rock scree we'd just scrambled. The mellow *tang-tang* of wooden bells, and barking of a guard dog ricocheted across the pasture. Though I couldn't see the flock, I could plainly hear their plaintive calls floating from a lower part of the hillside.

"There they are. See them? Ulpiano y *El Cazador*," Juanna pointed down the mountain and across the open valley.

I shook my head for all I could make out was a stand of three or four Rowan trees and faint wisp of smoke at least a couple of miles away. But I expect they spotted us the instant we appeared over the saddle outlined against the sky.

"Yahooo," we called waving frantically, though they couldn't hear us, and headed for the woodsmoke.

Digging our heels into soft earth of the downward slope, Anthony, Miles, and I raced past Juanna and Ed and waited breathless on the valley floor till they caught up. Walking the final distance together. We could see them plainly by then, and in thirty minutes more, and we sank to the grass beside them under the Rowan Trees up-wind from the fire's smoke.

"*Holá. Holá.* Have you been waiting long?" Ed asked.

But Ulpiano spoke not a word, played statue and never moved. Propped on one elbow stretched on his side, he stared right through us as if we weren't there.

Then, unable to keep his pose a second longer, he collapsed into laughter leaping to his feet, his eyes twinkling with pleasure.

"*Bienvenidos amigos,*" he grinned handing us his bota, and introduced his friend.

El Cazador waved a silent welcome intent on his cooking.

"*Conejo,*" he said simply, lifting the lid of two blackened pots when we strolled over to inspect.

El Cazador pushed a small branch deeper into the embers. Once they flared, he handed Anthony and Miles each a plate and set them to fan the fire.

Resting from our hike, we sprawled comfortably beneath the Rowans in the shade, when Ulpiano suddenly gave a shout.

"I can smell something. Quick all of you. Isabel, can you smell something? Right here, what can you smell?

"Rabbit? Garlic? Smoke...." I hesitated.

"What else? What else?" He was insistent.

"Umm, fresh air?"

"Go on. And? And...? Sniff again. What else? Go on, over here." He indicated the ground about three feet from the tree. "I can smell something. Put your nose there in that grass."

"Oregano? Clover? The earth?" He was clearly playing with me, but I was confused.

"What nothing else?" He and *El Cazador* collapsed. "Sniff harder." They laughed. But I'd run out of smells.

With a flip of his pocketknife, Ulpiano dug into a clump of grass and triumphantly pull out an earth-encrusted bottle of wine.

"What...?" Ed and I exclaimed, amazed. "How...?"

"And here, and here," *El Cazador* joined in materializing bottle after bottle from deep in the earth.

"*Milagro,*" Ulpiano filled each glass with its ruby-red liquid. "*Vino para beber.*"

Cool and fresh, the wine beat any I'd ever tasted. I closed my eyes and took another sip while Ulpiano intoned his favorite anti-priest toast.

"*Sangre de Christo,*" Ulpiano began. "*Muchos veces lo le visto...,* though I've seen your blood many times," he touched the base of his glass to his lips. "*Mais cuando le veo, yo solemente da una boleo.*" Imitating communicants receiving the Holy Communion, he whisked the glass away from his open mouth before he could take a sip. "*Salut.*" He jeered draining his glass. "We only get to kiss the glass while those *cabrónes* get to drink the wine."

A few moments of silence reigned while we digested the meaning.

"During our Civil War," *El Cazador* broke the silence. "I hid out on this mountain. So I never went thirsty again, I buried caches of wine all over this valley."

"Go on. Tell them the story." Ulpiano encouraged.

"In a village no more than twenty miles from here," indicating over the mountain, the hunter *El Cazador* began.

"I, and another partisan were taken prisoner and condemned to death by Franco's men. Our captors marched us out of the village at rifle point where they forced us to dig our own graves before they killed us. And while we did, those bastards lounged on the grass smoking and drinking they waved their bulging bota in our direction as we dug.

How about a last sip of wine, son's of whores? They taunted."

Varying his voice, miming vividly, and with dramatic pauses, *El Cazador* held us, his audience, in his grip.

"*If we are going to be shot,* I whispered to my compatriot, *let's make a run for it and at least die nobly in the attempt.*" His voice changed to a hushed rasp. "*You make a run for it into the woods and I'll run in the opposite direction to that clump of trees there. It's now or never. Ready? One, two, three, now.*"

El Cazador leaned forward and bellowed so forcefully I almost spilled my wine.

"Hollering and howling like a pack of wolves closing on their prey, we hurled our spades and clods of earth at them and streaked away. That startled them alright. Those Franco pigs didn't know which way to aim. Missed us both. I see the traitors in Cervera sometimes. When I do, I spit and turn my back. We never speak." He stared upwards, his face shadowed by the memory.

"Is that how you got your scar?" Miles questioned bluntly.

"That is another story." For a man who rarely spoke, it seemed he couldn't shut up.

Above the hunter's eyes and across his nose, mottled red lumps puckered his skin making it difficult not to stare.

"I'd been watching that eagle for a full year from a hollow I dug close to his eyrie. Late summer when it was large enough to hide in, I crouched inside to wait and covered my body with heather while he was away hunting. At last he hovered above me within reach. Leaping from my hiding place I caught him by the legs. Oh, but he was strong. Too strong for me. How he fought. One hour. Two, maybe three. My hold began to slip and…" The hunter looked at each of us in turn and suddenly gripped his own face with imaginary claws. "He managed to pull his left talon from my hand and clamp it over my face. I thought I was done for, so fearsome was his grip. Two hours it took me but little by little, claw by claw, I worked each talon free then let him go. I still had him by his other leg, see. As he soared into the air with a mighty beating of wings, I took to my heels and away. Once eagles capture their prey, they never let go, you see."

The boys' eyes widened as he mimed peeling each talon from his face. He should have been on the stage, his performance was so compelling.

"One day, I want to try again, to catch that proud king, and display him with my collection." *El Cazador*, hunter, taxidermist, fell silent then reaching for the whetstone cradled in the goat horn hanging from his waist, sharpened his knife with a killer's rapid strokes. No way would I want to be his adversary.

Reliving his adventure, he pulled the lethal blade towards his chest slicing translucent slivers of jamon onto a scrap of newspaper. Raw onion followed, then crusty slabs of *paisano* bread. Did he secretly devour eagle at home?

I truly believed him capable having seen the gruesome glass-eyed collection of stuffed birds and beasts in his home.

"*A comer.*" Ulpiano broke the spell. "But first more wine." He plunged his knife twice into the earth and fished out another perfect bottle. He knew exactly where to dig.

Course number two. Juanna unwrapped two tortillas she'd pre-cooked at home from half a dozen eggs beaten and baked with onion and potato. Still soft inside, eaten cold on a hot summer's day high in a mountain meadow, nothing tasted better.

Course three. Rabbit smothered in powdered sweet pimento, garlic, chile and parsley arrived next, ladled by Juanna onto our plates. Sopping the rich sauce with bread, every plate was soon wiped clean, every bone noisily sucked dry, fingers licked, the plates put away. There was something euphoric about food eaten in the wild, its smell, its texture and tang of mixed flavors on my tongue. Something freeing about the mountain air, Ulpiano threw a handful of grass at Juanna, and dodged when she threw a handful back. They laughed. We laughed. Every-one so happy.

I lay back in the high meadow grass beside the others and watched the clouds skim across the sky till my lids sagged. The men's voices faded and soon, they, and Juanna too, succumbed to sleep. Rolling onto my stomach when I awoke, to better scent the earth and sweet grass, I startled to see a field vole peering at me through the green. He stopped his chewing and twitched his nose. For a brief moment his pink eyes held mine before he scuttled away. Or did I dream his visit?

We left no trace of our picnic spot when we left for home. One behind the other, and set off by a narrow path I could barely make out. In less than a mile the path petered out, and we found ourselves on a steep rocky overgrown track of scrub trees and broom hemmed in by towering cliffs on either side. Slipping and slithering behind Ulpiano and *El Cazador*, focused on where next to place our feet, we all of us struggled to keep upright. Just as I was wondering why they'd chosen such a difficult route, poof, suddenly the two of them were gone. Vanished. Ulpiano and *El Cazador*. No sign of either man. Confused, we stopped not sure what to do. When out of nowhere, poof, Ulpiano reappeared from a bush fifteen or twenty feet above us, laughing, arms akimbo, his legs straddling two boulders.

"Up here. Come see," he called.

As we clambered over loose rocks to reach him, he disappeared through an almost invisible cleft behind a boulder calling us to follow. The boys first, in turn, we squeezed ourselves between the narrow opening and found ourselves in a narrow cave partly open to the sky that had clearly once been lived in.

"*Bienvenidos a mi casa*," *El Cazador* stood there in the dim light beside a bed of spongy bracken and heather laid over dried branches. Apart from a crate of rifle shells, a mug, plate, eating utensils, a battered kettle and frying-pan, the cave was bare.

"I cooked only at night, to hide the smoke. Until the war ended, this was my home for two long years," he paused. "After the war was over, I made damn sure I never again went without my wine. I buried bottles in here and all over the valley. See…" and *El Cazador* plunged his knife into the earth floor to reveal a stash of wine, before carefully covering it again. "Just in case…"

From the flash of violent way he used his knife I realized it was not the moment to hound him with questions. I wish I had, for I never did discover how he'd managed to keep hidden for so long, if his friends ever knew he was alive or knew of his hidey-hole; if he lived solely by his hunting; if anyone brought him supplies; if he was lonely and that was why he got into taxidermy? Did he catch and stuff little birds, rabbits, and other wild creatures to keep around him for company?

I still have the photo, Ulpiano and *El Cazador* outside their hideout, wine bottle and glasses in hand, broadly smiling.

18

IGNACIO

Celebrating our arrival with Juan in the meadow before putting up our tents as we usually did, that fifth summer we were surprised to see Mariano hurrying towards us. No smile of greeting, his face solemn, he took Ed by the arm and pulled him aside to the sheep pen beyond the gate and away from the children and me.

"I have bad news. Ignacio is dead," he said simply. And they'd embraced and clung to each other and wept and hugged and wept as they stood together in the sheep pen up to their ankles in straw.

Red eyed, Ed returned alone to the tent where I anxiously waited. Wondering. Worrying. Running a hundred scenarios in my head that never included Ignacio's tragic death.

"What's happened to your legs," I'd exclaimed in horror momentarily distracted.

Black, both lower legs crawled with sheep fleas so thick, I thought at first some dreadful disease had affected his skin.

Not everything about Spain was perfect. We were away when Ignacio died. I've had to fill in the sad details myself and run the story again and again in my head till the horror of it lessoned with its repeating.

Ignacio. His story.

A sixth glass followed a fifth. Alejandro's world, rosy as the *clarete* splashing from the chipped china jug, filled a final glass, one more than his evening's quota. The embossed image of La Virgin on the jug's surface, gazed at him so sorrowfully he bowed his head.

"*Coño*," he swore. "Okay. Okay," he conceded, and hurled the contents at the flaming logs.

That evening like so many since his brother passed, he drank alone, the silence broken by Madre's heavy breathing and the fire's sudden hiss. He'd help her off to bed soon enough. He let her doze.

From the fire's flicker, Ignacio, materialized to sit with them just as real as when he lived, his charcoal eyes glowing like a devil risen from hell.

Alejandro grabbed a stick.

"*Vete*. Go," he growled and lunging at the flames disassembled the apparition.

Madre's lips pursed, sucking in her sleep. Her head hung awkwardly slumped on her chest. A snake of silver hair trailed over her shoulder glittering in the firelight.

A sudden blast of rain and sleet rattled the windowpane causing Alejandro to look nervously over his shoulders.

"Ignacio," he shivered. "…back from the dead." He rubbed his arms and fed a small length of beech into the fire to keep it alive a little longer.

Memories of Ignacio persisted…his agonized nine-year old screams…the struggle of the family and neighbors to release his trapped arm from the threshing machine's grinding jaws…the mangled mess, the bone, blood. The clumsy repair leaving his hand twisted, fingers stiffly curved, a useless claw, Ignacio, forever relegated to women's work in the fields, and the house, was demoted to sweep, cook and rake in the fields.

His self-esteem shattered, he took to drink and women. Married women. Women who would keep their secret and held no expectation of a long commitment.

From the age of eighteen, sniffing out the sex-starved, Ignacio lifted the skirt of many. For days at a time, he vanished, returned disheveled, his eyes less wild, his lips less curled, and words less bitter than when he'd left.

With his oil-slicked hair uncovered, his button down collared shirts, his tongue loosened with rum cuba-libres, Ignacio told lewd jokes to anyone who'd listen; Catholics, Protestants, upper bar, lower bar, a philanderer, he wasn't fussy, he earned his reputation in the village as a "fancy-man."

Alejandro sighed. Counted his fingers. One. Two...yes it had been two long years since his brother died.

He thought back to when Ignacio turned forty and took himself off to a hospital in Palencia, the capital town of the Castilian Province, sixty miles away to get his hand fixed, and become whole again. A surgeon volunteered to operate. *For free* he'd said. Ignacio jumped at the offer.

The operation was successful, the message related more than a week later. He'd taken the letter to Gusto, the sheepherder, the only man in the village who wore glasses, the only man able to read.

He didn't come home right away. Rehabilitation would keep Ignacio away for four and a half months. News of his good progress traveled by word of mouth.

He'll be here in within the week, so get cooking Ma. How about his favorite, that special rabbit you make so well?" He suggested.

All smiles, he looked at her questioningly. Yes, it would be good having his brother home again he'd missed his brother.

Since they'd heard the news, their spirits lifted. He could see it in his mother's, La Madre's, eyes, in the way she hopped up and down the stairs like a woman ten years less her age. She even seemed to sit a little straighter.

Three, four days ticked by, then late one night after the two of them had long been asleep, Alejandro started up in bed.

"We've brought your brother home." Two strangers hammered on the door late one night, shouting up, throwing stones at the windows.

"*Holá. Holá.* Your brother's home," the men kept the stones hailing till Alejandro roused from his bed.

"Wake up Madre. Ignacio has come." Alejandro bounded down the stairs shouting in excitement.

"Welcome back. Welcome home," he flung wide the outer door to the courtyard.

Two men stood silent beside their van.

"My brother….?" Alejandro faltered.

Gestured towards the back. His face covered by a cloth, Ignacio lay stiff on a stretcher. Dead. No advance notice. No explanation.

The van's drivers read the death certificate.

> SEX: Male
> NAME: Ignacio Anton don Roldan
> DATE OF BIRTH: July 5th, 1937.
> DATE OF DEATH: January 10th, 1977.
> CAUSE OF DEATH: complications following surgery.
> ADDRESS: Ruesga Village, Palencia.

"Murderers. Murderers. *Hijos de putas.* Sons of whores." He roared. "What have you done to him?" Punching the air, Alejandro wailed for his brother.

Madre, her hair loosened, a shawl pulled about her nightshirt padded into the kitchen. The lighted candle trembling in her hand illuminated a plain coffin on the floor. Madre's cries, his own, a wildfire of agony torching the dark.

"My son. My beloved," Madre collapsed wailing, and threw her body across the wooden box.

"Delivers of death," she screamed after them as they scuttled down the stairs and fled into the night.

Alejandro jabbed the embers extinguishing the last flames, his flashback, and the flickering of Ignacio's smile.

"*Vete*—Be gone." One final jab at the ash and Alejandro forced himself to his feet.

"Come, Madre. Bedtime. Come."

Reaching for his mother's hand, Alejandro gently pulled her awake and walked with her to one of two low, glass-paned doors leading directly off the landing opposite the kitchen.

Madre's bedroom. His. No windows to the outside, the air hung warm, wood ash, pungent garlic, pork, beans. He heard her piss hit the enamel of her chamber pot, the soft thump of her canvas slippers on the floor, the squeak of wire springs.

Two solitary brass bedsteads, two cubes of darkness, Alejandro missed his brother. He checked Madre's door stood ajar, waited to hear his mother's breath before entering his room.

Alejandro sank onto the mattress beside the yawning depression parallel to his own on Ignacio's side of the bed parallel to his own, his palm resting where Ignacio's belly should have been. Brothers, both in their late forties, they'd shared a bed their whole lives.

He lay still, straining for the sound of his mother's breathing filtering through the dividing wall. Alejandro inhaled, exhaled. Matched the rhythm of his breath to hers till their breathing synchronized. Comforted, his eyes closed.

But while he slept, Ignacio's women paraded his dreams taunting milk-white buttocks, fleshy thighs, spread legs, a taste of warm softness, and an ecstasy of relief he'd only experienced in secret with a goat, and his cow, the beautiful Princessa.

That is my imaginary version of Ignacio's death, the impact on his family. A hollow never to be refilled.

Ignacio's absence hung over that summer though his name nor his death was not mentioned again.

19

MARIANO

I own just one blurry photo of Mariano, the gentle man who married into Ruesga's Anton Family, but in my mind the image of his face, pale and shy as an albino moon, is as clear as any snapshot in my album.

My first memory of him is seeing his hazy phantom emerge from the dark cavern opening off Alejandro's cowshed. Like a rat by its tail, he carried a foot-long link of *chorizo* still glistening from the vat of oil in which it had been preserved. But, alarmed by coming suddenly upon us gathered in Alejandro's hallway with his two brother-in-laws, Alejandro and Ignacio, sharing a glass of wine, he melted back into the *quadro* without a word.

Two years more years would pass for him to more than shyly nod if we came upon each other unawares. But all that changed once

Ed and I began helping out in the fields, and we'd shared his family's fiesta meal together.

To meet him he looked no different from any other man in the village apart from his lack of tan. Same dust-stained ill-fitting navy pants, dirt-ingrained shirt, faded canvas shoes, and black felt *boina* clamped to his head. But unlike his brothers and friends, who broadcast their anti-fascist leanings by wearing their beret tipped firmly left, Mariano hid his political allegiance by planting his firmly centered.

A sort of misfit unsuited to heavy farm work with his gentle ways, Mariano married into the Anton family owning not a field, nor single cow. Almost reclusive, I never saw Mariano in any bar. Never encountered him wandering the village or joining in at Fiesta. Like a captive tortoise, he withdrew into his shell rarely venturing beyond his *quadro*, except to ferry milk and eggs the two short lanes between his and La Madre's, his Mother-in-law's house, or occasionally emerge at harvest time to help out.

So, if we felt like seeing him, we went to him, to his and Manuella's house by the river., a five minute walk from Alejandros's.

Peering round the massive wooden gateway to his yard, I'd catch him sitting in the stripe of shade along the wall of his house cradling a rabbit, and whispering aloud whatever thoughts flitted from inside his head. To his pigs, chickens, milking goats, precious bees, even the swallows nesting in the eaves and thieving sparrows.

When I sing, my chickens give me eggs, he nodded knowingly, his eyes wide.

I nodded smiling at the picture of him crooning.

One early evening, the boys and I called round to show him a grasshopper they'd caught. Examining it he threw it free into the air to save it from his rooster.

"*Bete. Bete,*" Mariano warned the bird away, scooping up a handful of dirt but not throwing it.

The princely rooster arched his neck, and with one final defiant crow, stalked off to join his harem.

In the settling silence I looked around. A rickety balcony teetered dangerously from the upper floor of his and Manuella's timbered house and there set into the granite wall below the red roof-tiles I noticed the ends of three hollowed logs daubed in place with clods of plaster and mud.

"What are those for, Mariano?" I asked noticing drilled holes patterning each capped end.

"They're for my bees," he explained slowly staring at me as if I was simple. "The bees fly through those holes and make their honey inside the logs."

"*Ven*," he stood beckoning us. "I show you."

Following him into the house up the wooden stairway and through a smoke blackened kitchen, we crowded into the small side room he called his bodega between a cluster of wooden oil vats, a couple of wine flagons, and encrusted wine bottles.

I could hardly move for the bunches of dried herbs, a couple of willow baskets, and Mariano's leather *bota* dangling from its beetle-pockmarked and cobweb festooned beams without banging my head. A storehouse for spiders more like, I shuddered brushing a clinging strand from my face.

"There," he indicated, pulling off a wooden cover from one of the embedded hollow logs jutting from the wall, "*Mosca's de miel*. I take their honey from here if I ask them."

Windowless and hot from sunbaked roof tiles I fought for breath obediently peering at the slabs of honeycomb clinging to the hollow inside. Opening his mouth and sticking out his tongue Mariano mimed catching the dripping honey.

Born the wrong time, the wrong place, Mariano would have been a vegetarian, a botanist or naturalist by choice. Killing for the table he left to his wife, Manuella, and turned pale when she set him to pluck and gut a chicken.

What kind of a man are you, I'd once heard her sneer. Twice his width, stocky legged, a floral scarf over her too short hair, Manuella glared.

Poor Mariano, she treated him like a child. Her supercilious sniffs at the mention of his name, made it clear she'd not only married beneath her, but it was his fault she was childless, and flin-flan the rabbits performed so casually was beyond him. But she did have a softer side.

"When I met Mariano, he'd been a Guardia de Seville for two years," she blurted suddenly one afternoon.

For once Manuella stayed sat with us in the *quadro*.

For a brief second, Manuella's eyes softened remembering the young soldier she married. She looked up at him almost admiringly, then with a shake of her head, reached out, and grabbing a passing hen, roughly plunged a finger up its feathered orifice and announced, "*Huevo vienne.*"

Mariano, suddenly shy, glanced in her direction. Clearly he adored her, though I rarely saw her return his affection.

"They gave me a whistle when they took me away and made me a Guardia." Mariano announced continuing our earlier conversation as if it were still ongoing. "*Whooo. Whooo,*" he mimed.

Shyly anxious, he caught his wife's eye for silent permission before beginning.

"*Sigue,*" she beamed and told him to go on

We stared at him amazed to hear him so talkative.

"I was seventeen," he began, "when a big lorry stopped at my house with people in the back. Two Guardia pointing rifles leaped out.

Arriba! You're to come with us, they commanded. *No need to bring anything. Get in.*

Me, and this many others," Mariano paused holding up all ten fingers and thumbs, "and those two Guardia with guns. Carlito from my school was in the back. He rolled his eyes to say hello when I got in, but I was too frightened to answer back."

As in the documentary I'd once seen, they dragged gentle seventeen-year-old Mariano from his widowed mother's side and threw him in beside his friend in the back. I couldn't imagine their terror at being forcibly driven away from the sheltered village where he was born.

"They shouted," Mariano continued. "*In case you cabrónes have ideas of running away.*" Mariano pointed an imaginary pistol recalling the scene.

"The lorry went so fast it blew cold," he shivered acting out his memory.

"Like me, lots of us were sick over the side but they wouldn't let us stop the whole day until they finally let us out to sleep on the ground and eat. The bread they gave us with the cheese and chorizo was full of grit but I was so hungry, I swallowed it down with some *clarete*.

The road went straight the next day and flat like Madre's rolled bread before it rises. I felt better. There was no more road left after the edge of Spain because the land fell into a field of water."

Out, the Guardia yelled. *Training Camp.* They pulled me out onto the ground. They didn't wait for me to get down.

After they shaved our heads and took away our clothes, I had to put on big boots, and a green uniform with red tabs here and here." Mariano pointed to both collars.

"We had to march around with pretend rifles on our shoulders and stamp our boots. The chief shouted when I bumped into some-one. He shouted in my ear, and because I couldn't shoot a wooden man he took away my gun. He gave me a whistle instead. *Blow, tonto, blow, stupid,* he ordered.

I was glad when he sent me to a town with more houses than Potes. They told me to blow my whistle and make the cars and lorries go round and round."

"*Whooo-whooo,*" Mariano pursed his lips and blew.

I almost laughed out loud as he leaned forward from his waist holding his imaginary whistle between his lips, and performed frantic semaphore-like signals directing invisible traffic with his hands.

His innocent simplicity captivated me. His way of telling. A country boy who'd barely seen a car. The chaos. The choking bot-tlenecks he must have caused. *Unbelievable.* I shook my head. *What a scene.*

Whooo-whooo, Mariano blew again, his left hand up and arm held straight out in front of him.

Stop. Start. Go left. Go right, his arms gesticulated wildly re-en-acting his roll.

"My whistle made all the cars stop. And when I waved the cars and lorries went round and round. Except for Sunday, I had to stand in the middle of four roads and blow my whistle." Mariano sighed recalling his aloneness.

I pictured him, a country boy, in an ill-fitting uniform who'd barely seen a car standing on a podium under an umbrella enjoying, his newfound power.

"They called Sunday 'stand down' time, but I had nothing to do. So every week I walked four miles to the town and sat in the square on a bench under a Tila tree to talk to the pigeons. They flew down and pecked breadcrumbs like my chickens do back home while I told them stories about my Madre being so far away, and how the goats gave her milk to drink, and the soft cheese she made. The pigeons liked me talking to them. They sang *coo-coo* to stop me feeling sad.

For two summers and two winters I was a Guardia. Then in March a man called me to the barracks and took away my whistle and my uniform. *Here, go home,* they told me one day, *...your clothes, a ticket and a hundred pesetas. You can keep your boots. You're discharged.*

The train whistled at every station till it came to Santander. I got out, and caught a bus through the mountains to Potes and walked home. Madre cried when she saw me. *You're so thin, you've been gone so long.*"

Mariano looked at me, his eyes watery.

"You did a very important job as Guardia." I smiled.

Suddenly bashful, he got up and scuttled back to the safety of his *quadro.*

A week passed before we saw him again and when we did, he had a curious request.

"Can I come with you when you next go swimming? Not to swim, but to watch. Is it like frogs?" he asked, "I've never actually seen a person swim."

And why would he have, I lectured myself, never having seen a swimming pool.

Same as everyone growing up in the mountains around, he feared deep water. Feared Ruesga would be swallowed up, its people, animals, the fields, trees, and every small hamlet, as the reservoir had swallowed the village beyond the dam where his cousin once lived.

"At night I dreamed water spilled over the *presa* and crept towards my house to drown Manuella and me in our bed, and suck away my cows, my pigs and chickens before I could save them. I saw my bees rise like a cloud searching for somewhere to go. And I cried so loud, Manuella had to wake me."

His eyes swept over the reservoir's expanse of water, so threatening to him, so beckoning to us. We saw space where he saw death.

"People in the village won't go near," Mariano looked serious.

"Just put your toe in, Mariano," Miles and Anthony encouraged. But he stayed watching us from the road.

We spread our towels on the sloped ground we called "our beach." Excited to show off, Anthony and Miles waded the shallows to a partially submerged ship-shaped rock perhaps ten feet from the shoreline then launched into the air and with a mighty splash and disappeared below the water.

"Oh. Oh," Mariano wailed. "They've gone." He clutched his head unable to watch until their two heads sprung into sight.

"My cousin lies up there. His grave is drowned." Still shaking, and clearly distressed, Mariano pointed at the liquid valley.

"Some evenings when the moon is full, I hear the church bells tolling," Mariano, sadly continued, "and my cousin…I hear his voice with the other dead crying for their loved ones."

I wished he hadn't told me for I immediately pictured the grisly opened graves he described, the strewn headstones and bleached bones of ghostly skeletons trapped forever, wandering in their sunken graveyard.

His fear got me thinking. All too frequently heavy rainstorms swelled the reservoir's level and forced its waters through jagged cracks in the wall. Though there'd never been a major leak, I dreaded to think of the devastation if the dam had broken.

Mariano still standing on the road above the beach refused to step nearer. He waited till all four of us were in the water before he left. As I pushed from shore and floated on my back, I saw him scuttle across the dam as if it might crumble beneath his feet.

Days slid by, and all too soon September would be upon us. I propelled myself away from shore and pushed the thought away.

20

ROSITA'S BODEGA

"Here? This? This is the Bar?" Stepping over the trail of round green cowpats splashed on the cobblestones, I hesitated.

The boys and I drooped having dragged after Ed and his wild drinking buddy, Nano, to and from every bar in town. Late afternoon, the cobblestones burned like coals. I badly needed to get off my feet.

Though Nano had explained only a few locals knew the exact location, this surely this couldn't be the place. A laden wooden cart creaked slowly past shedding wisps of hay onto the narrow street. More like a barnyard with its crowded mix of crumbling barns and shuttered lofts, I grumbled under my breath. Nano must surely have got it wrong.

"*Sí. Rosita's. Ándele,*" Nano urged me to keep moving, clicking the iron latch and pushing open the rough wooden door.

"*Que passa? Aqui estamos,*" he urged me again charging ahead with Ed.

Lowering my head below the oak lintel, the boys I followed them into a dim, windowless room. The soured whiff of wine spills, acrid saltpeter rising from a *metcha*'s smoldering yellow cord, I watched a man light his fag. Cheap tobacco, smoke and olive oil, the foul mix of odors blanketed the air.

The single bulb burning below the fly-spotted plastic ceiling shade did nothing to brighten the room, nothing to disguise its grease-blackened walls, the death-spotted and browned fly-paper, the unwashed flagstone floor littered with husks of sunflower seeds, *pipas*, nut shells and olive pits. Now grey, the once purple oregano, thyme, and yellow flowers of *te*, the faded bundles of wild herbs strung on the overhead beam only emphasized the gloom of decay. Mercedes warning to me flashed from earlier in the day.

"*La Cascarita?* Rosita's Bodega? It's no more than a brothel, she'd sniffed when I mentioned where Nano planned taking us that evening to sample *avellanas*, hazel cobs. Then with a look added, "That low-down place is not suitable for you or the children."

I glanced around taking in the scene, the two benches, and rough hand-hewn tables. Backs pasted the rough stonewalls both sides of the room, Rosita's regulars, men not many other bars welcomed, clutched his own *poron de rosado*. A *boina,* a black felt beret anchored every man's head to the left ear proclaimed their opposition to El Generalissimo Franco, the Catholic Church with her loathed Priests. I cursed myself for not bringing my Brownie to capture the Hogarth tableau straight from one of his prints.

"*Bienvenidos,*" Rosita greeted surprised seeing us crowd into the room's small space. "*Aqui.*" Her scarlet lips split into a smile plumping and wrinkling the two rouged circles painted on her cheeks.

"Sit here," she indicated one of three marble-topped tables set in the middle of the room, sweeping the previous occupants' scattering of crumbs to the floor.

"*Vino. Bocarones,*" Nano called loudly flashing a handful of *peseta* notes and coins before we'd even taken our seats. No wonder people nicknamed Nano, *Le Furia,* the Tornado, talked of his stories, passed on the rumors…all the women he bedded…a secret child… his drinking…his crazy behaviors like the time he ploughed up one of Juan's fields in the middle of the night to repay a favor. Drunk of course. And outraged, the village had woken to see the hillside wildly scarred by criss-crossed furrows. But Nano was handsome. Loveable. A hunk of a man and charming, with his blonde curls and dangerously carefree manner. Despite his one opaque red-veined eye, like most every female, I found him a real looker. And he knew it.

As my eyes adapted to the gloom, I was surprised to recognize a few of the customers. Ramon. Oscar. El Rey, and a couple of other men I'd seen lurking in the corners of some of Ed and Nano's favorite watering holes.

"*Buenas,*" I nodded to Ramon, El Boracho, the drunk, trying not to recoil. Poor man with his purple suppurating, bulbous nose, slurred speech and tattered clothes, his drunkenness made him difficult to be around. Ashamedly, like me, most people dismissed him, and, revolted, turned their backs. So used to rejection, when he saw I greeted him, he looked away and took a gulp of wine. Pink sapphire, the liquid inside his poron shimmered, splashing a rare ray of beauty into the squalor.

Oscar, another loner I knew by sight from the bullfights, nodded in our direction. I hardly recognized him at first without the uniform he always wore; the immaculate white trousers and shirt, the scarlet cummerbund and kerchief round his neck. But at a bullfight he transformed to a whip-cracking charioteer driving his team of three mules into the ring between corridas. The gates swung open, and like Ben Hur in he charged at full gallop enveloped in a cloud of dust to the cheers of the crowd. With a clatter of chains and tackle Oscar leapt to the ground, harnessed the bull by its horns, and dragged its carcass from sight. Sadly people avoided him socially for a smell of death, of abattoir's blood hung about him.

I caught the eye of el Rey, nicknamed ironically for his stature and attire. We stared at each other. Rude, I know but I couldn't help myself. Four feet in height, el Rey rattled loose inside a too-big overcoat. Frayed and patched, its hem trailed heavy like the ermine trim of a royal cape along the ground. Rolled up sleeves, thick fur cuffs completed his kingly image. His eyes stayed locked with mine. I shifted, trapped. Here I was, a woman, a rare moth unexpectedly inside his male domain. Eyes, creepy, fixed on mine, he leered a nicotine-coffee-stained smile revealing two rows of pointy milk-teeth he'd kept since childhood. Slowly, he raised one doll-sized hand, waggled his baby fingers in my direction. I turned away.

"*Uno pincha, de anchovas,*" Rosita plunked down a small saucer of anchovies awash in oil spiked with toothpicks, and a hunk of bread on the marble table top in front of us.

Sitting there, I made the mistake of drumming my hands on the underside of the marble tabletop. My fingernails sank into a thick film of grease. I shuddered thinking of the many years it must have taken to accumulate those layers. Not a paper napkin in sight, I quickly wiped my hand using the hem of my skirt.

Un-self-conscious of his mottled eyeball, Nano swiveled his good eye to Rosita's daughter behind the bar.

"Delfina, Delfina, *te amo,*" he reached imploringly towards her, and with a shake of his golden curls, tilted back his head and broke into song. With a brief arch of both eyebrows I watched her pause, steady, then continue to pour the wine she was decanting from a chipped ceramic jug into a *poron* and hand it to her mother.

If he hoped to impress Rosita's daughter, Delfina's attention, he failed. She slid from view into the bodega with a tray of unwashed glasses without a glance in his direction.

"Now be quiet. Be a good boy." Giving him a shove Rosita couldn't hide her smile.

It was plain to me from their easy banter the two were long-time friends despite, or because of, the twenty years between them. Rosita and Nano, outcasts both. Watching their dance, I saw them as a pair of eagles unfettered by earth's gravity soaring where ever the wind carried them. I wished could be as free.

Immediately I liked her. No grand airs or pretense about her. Take her or leave her, Rosita simply was. Plumped up, an aged flamenco dancer, all I could do was stare. No black garb, headscarf, cover-all housecoat, or peasant canvas shoes like local women, she flouted her curves in a black and orange belted full-skirt and puff-sleeved blouse. I wanted to imprint her image. The mane of her straight coal black hair, oiled and coiled into an untidy chignon low on the nape of her neck, the whiteness of her facial make-up, her panda mascara-blackened eyes, her jangly gypsy earrings and the scarlet arched bows of her lipstick. A bird of paradise trapped in a dingy cage, misjudged as a whore only from the way she dressed and the misfortune of having loved a double dealing bounder who left her with child.

But it was not Rosita's attention, but her daughter's, Delfina's he sought. Rumored to be the illicit child of a famous bullfighter her mother had fallen for, tall and slim, Delfina held herself with the arrogant carriage of a Toreador. No wonder Nano chased her.

Undeterred by her outward scorn, stomping, clapping the beat, Nano raised his voice and put on a performance worthy of a peacock seeking a mate. Though gone from sight, he knew Delfina heard him. Thumping footsteps across the ceiling, and bangs upstairs broadcast she wasn't far. Secretly, on moonless nights when no one was around to point fingers, I wondered if she sometimes succumbed to his advances.

Still showing off, Nano ordered a slice of Rosita's *del casa tortilla*, blood sausage and *chorizo*, and more wine.

"*Rosado*," Rosita beamed placing a *poron* of *clarete* handle towards me with its spout facing away. "*Primera.*"

Tilting my head back as far as I was able, I raised the poron over my head at arms-length. The pink stream exploded on my tongue and dribbled down my chin.

"Go on swallow. Swallow," Nano laughed.

"Hopeless," I lamented passing it on. Unlike the boys and Ed, I never mastered open-mouthed swallowing in all the eleven summers we spent in Spain

"Like this," El Furia demonstrated.

Bending and straightening his arm never spilling a drop, his Adam's apple sawing up and down, the pale liquid cascaded neatly down his throat.

"*Olé. Olé.*" We cheered.

"*Ahora, avellanas,*" Ten minutes later, Nano called to Rosita asking for a *medio* kilo of the cobnuts for which her bar was famed. Just in time, for a group of four men spilled through the door loudly demanding the same.

Scooped straight from the charcoal burner onto a cast iron pair of scales I watched Rosita carefully balance the bell-shaped brass weights, subtracting and adding individual nuts till the scales swung level.

"*Ahora,*" she tipped the cobs onto our table and materializing six brick-sized blocks of wood from under her arms, dumped them on the table.

"*Quema. Cuidado.*" Too hot to touch, hands on hips, she stood back chortling at our confusion.

"*Como esso,*" she demonstrated, grabbing a block and smashing it down on a single cobnut and cracking its *cascara* neatly in two.

Bang, smash, laughing, we followed her lead pounding our blocks and scattering nuts and shells across the marble tabletop and onto the floor.

"*No, no, suave menos fuerte. Assi,*" seeing our mess of powdered shells and kernels, she and Nano neatly cracked open the shells releasing unbroken kernels again and again.

It took much laughter and practice before being rewarded with any piece worth eating.

The bar erupted to raucous noise as we vied with the newly arrived customers to make ourselves heard over the din. No point speaking. Breaking every British rule, I tried a cautious loud *Olé*. No-one even looked my way. I opened my mouth and yelled to my boys, *this is fun, isn't this fun?* They looked up smiling, but I don't think they heard.

"She keeps a knife hidden in her clothing," Nano lowered his voice addressing Ed nodding towards Rosita. "Only folk who don't know her call her *La Puta*, the whore, and are foolish enough to make a pass."

I turned casually to study her clothing pretending not to be listening. Where, I wondered to myself? Clearly not in the deep crevasse of her cleavage, for a good expanse of her ample flesh spilled from the frilly neckline of her blouse. Perhaps a blade strapped by a garter high on her thigh?

"A man from the next village once ran his hand over her rump, and forcing his fist between her legs asked how much for *flin-flan*. Big mistake. *A la calle, hijo-de-puta.*" Curling his lips, exposing his teeth, Nano demonstrated, continuing his tale. "*Colibra* she screeched Hearing her mother, Delfina, grabbed the shepherd's crook hanging above the bar and leapt to mother's side. A knife pressed to the transgressor's throat, in a flash, Rosita pried the son-of-a-whore out of her bar and onto the cobblestone before he knew what was happening." Nano paused. "The wilder the stories the better," he laughed. "Nobody's touched her since."

La Cascarita, Rosita's bodega, was no more a brothel than Rosita was the Madam. I saw her as motherly from the way she treated her regulars, kind even. I once saw her unwrap a square of newsprint filled with filched scraps of cheese and leftover ham from a paying customer's order, and place it before El Rey knowing his pockets held only used cigarette butts, Rizla paper and a length of string. I never once saw her disappear into the backroom with any man. Her regular customers consisted of the town's tragic rejects. Too old, too destitute to cause her trouble, too frail and dried up to more than dream, more fascinated by their wine, Rosita's rounded breasts and buttocks no longer stirred them.

"Please, please let the *Cascarita* be the same," I'd silently pray when we visited her each summer.

Pushing open the door, I'd give a sigh of relief. There in the gloom weighing a batch of hazels stood Rosita as plump and gaudily painted as ever. Rushing towards us with an ear-splitting screech, breath-squeezing hugs and cheek-pinchings of welcome, she brought Delfina running from behind the bodega's curtain. I looked around. No fancy tablecloths, no bright lighting, the familiar row of sad customers still clutched their wine. The crash-bang of nut-cracking and noisy fun, the fetid air, it was as if we'd never stepped away.

21

THE DAY THE COW DIED

I couldn't define it, but something felt off that Wednesday. For a start the normally busy Bar Juanon stood eerily empty when Ed and I swung by there for a drink after a hot morning by the lake. Thirsty, but not in any hurry, glad for its cooling darkness, we leaned on the bar's granite slab waiting for somebody to serve us. One, two, five minutes and still not a soul in sight.

"*Holá. Holá,*" Ed called, but only a hollow *holá* echoed back from the walls.

"Weird. Where can everybody be?" I commented aloud.

We were just about to give up and head for our tents to make lunch, when Upe, Juan and Mercedes' daughter, scurried from the kitchen, a harried frown furrowing her normally cheerful face.

At the very same instant, the doorway darkened, and there in the midst of a jostling crowd of men I saw Juan surrounded by a group of his men friends herding him into the bar. Arms slung about his shoulders, slapping one another's backs and talking at full volume, they swamped the empty space crowding us into a corner.

No smiles, no *holás*, in our direction. With the briefest glance, Upe wordlessly slid two vinos in our direction and handing two lemonades to the boys, quickly turned back to serve her father and his friends.

I raised my eyebrows at Ed unable to believe what I was seeing as she reached for a bottle of the best brandy normally reserved for fiestas and poured her father a glass of the *Presidente Veijo*. Juan never drank as far as I knew, let alone slug hard liquor as he did that day. And at midday? Not once, but three times I watched Upe fill the line of brandy balloons she'd set along the bar.

"Bien, eh? Todo bien, amigo?" Juan's friends kept up their back slapping cheer and checked how their friend was doing.

More a statement than a question, raising their glasses over and over, they thundered rapid toasts trapping their friend at the bar. Not looking at them directly, Juan assented with a grunt. He did not look a happy man. Barely audible, his answers monosyllabic and forced, Juan's cheeks blazed red. His eyes glowed bloodshot.

I pretended not to be spying, although I was of course. Curious to know what the hell was going on I cupped my ears straining to make sense of their bellowed conversation. I shook my head defeated by the wall of noise.

Exactly what words passed between Juan and his friends, I hadn't enough Spanish to understand exactly, but from their body language, they clearly wanted no-one near their friend.

"Ed, we should leave. Something's up with Juan. Whatever do you think is going on. It's so unlike him to drink like that." I shouted in English. "It's not okay for us to be here. And anyway, I can't hear a word over all that noise."

"You're right. Let's go." Ed drained his *vino* in a gulp

That evening when we returned to meet up with Alejandro and Leandro, neither Mercedes or Juan were anywhere to be seen. No explanation, no welcome, her face mask-like, once again Upe served us in silence from behind the bar. It was impossible for me to read what she was thinking let alone feeling. Nor did I ask. Apart from us, the bar stayed eerily deserted. No point staying, we left some coins on the bar and turned to go. Following us to the door, Upe bolted it shut behind us.

"I'm off to say hello to La Madre," I called to Ed, before setting off to her house. Speaking a little more Spanish at last, I felt comfortable enough around the family to visit with them in their *quadro*.

I just reached the end of the lane and was passing the Juanon, when I almost collided into Mercedes hurrying by with a wooden scrubbing board clasped beneath her arm.

"*Voy al rio con la ropa,*" Mercedes paused staring at the ground, "*Um vaca de Juan's ha mourio ayer,*" she announced awkwardly without elaborating or offering an explanation for her husband's strange behavior the previous day.

"Oh. How dreadful. I'm so sorry," I fumbled lamely not finding fitting words to cover the loss of a cow.

Mercedes half-smiled, apologetic, before scurrying away to the river.

"*Holá. Holá, Madre,*" I called pushing open the giant *quadro* door and stepping into her enclosed yard.

Head bent forward and her eyes semi-closed in pleasure, I found the old lady sitting passively on an upturned bucket in front of her daughter, and Manuella gently brushing out her mother's silver-grey locks. Manuella stood at arm's length weaving La Madre's hair into a thick snake-like pigtail so long, it reached to her waist before she coiled and pinned it to a neat chignon low against the nape of her neck.

I lowered myself onto a nearby log to watch. Mother, daughter, their faces relaxed, the love they shared for each other the scene was beautiful to see. Usually so harshly practical, I looked at Manuella anew, saw the glow of kindness beneath her exterior. The sun pricked soft on my skin. The rooster crowed to his harem. Hens clucked scratching the dirt. A cow bell clunked. I could have sat forever.

"*Ahora. Esta. Finito.*" Manuella patted her mother's shoulder interrupting my reverie.

"Your hair looks nice," I admired.

We sat chatting awhile enjoying the sunshine.

"Did you hear about Juan's cow dying? Manuella, tell Isabel what happened." La Madre encouraged, eager to re-hear every gory detail again.

With that Manuella launched into her version of yesterday's drama. I couldn't understand all she said but I followed the meaning.

"I heard it from Emilio's wife herself," Manuella paused looking from me to her mother.

Unlike her to be so talkative, I could see Manuella preen.

"Yesterday was Emilio's turn to take the village milkers to pasture. Just a regular morning no different than any other, he and his son, Thatcho were sitting near the old coal mine watching the cows, when whoosh, quick as that," Manuella waved her hand, "Whoosh, a grey lobo streaked from the disused mine shaft right through the grazing herd and scarpered away over the mountain. Set the cows off mooing and running for their lives scattering them all over. It took Emilio and Thatcho the best part of an hour to round them up. That's when they found her, Juan's Bella. The poor creature's leg bone stuck out through her hide. Must have slipped and fallen in all the panic." Manuella bent her elbow at an awkward angle.

"*Malo. Malo.*" La Madre shook her head before urging Manuella to continue.

"That's it. Emilio sent his boy to get help. You know the rest." Manuella teased her mother pretending to stop.

"Bella was just lying there on her side panting and rolling her eyes, and moaning by the time Juan and two of his mates got to her. Nothing for it but to finish her off. Even with two sticks bound to her leg, and all for all their pulling, they couldn't get Juan's cow to her feet. Poor Juan. He knew what he had to do. Apparently, and I got this from Emilio's wife," Manuella raised her arms. "*Dios. Ayuda me, Mi pobre Bella.* Half choking, Juan buried his face against the softness of Bella's neck. Then, before he lost courage, smashed a rock against the soft spot on her skull...you know, same as in the bullfights. Killed her instantly. Poor man. He let out such an unearthly sound he set the ravens wheeling."

"*Pues finito.*" Manuella shrugged dusting her hands together.

"Horrible. Horrible. What guts it must have taken him to end her suffering." I muttered unable to get the horrific image out of my mind—Juan having to kill an animal he trained and worked with her whole life since he brought her into the world.

Now I understood. No wonder Juan behaved so strangely the day before. That he downed those couple of brandies, and his friends surrounded him with forced jollity never allowing him to be alone with his grief.

With the feeling I'd mislaid something, I felt a sudden twinge halfway between envy and regret for the indestructible bond these village people shared, the sense of belonging that I'd never experienced except with my children. I wanted what they had.

22

WINDOW OF HEAVEN

Though I've forgotten why, one summer after we'd been visiting
Ruesga for several years, we skipped our trip to Spain. It was April,
I remember, a wild spring evening in the mid seventies and the children were still children, young and vulnerable, we set sail for Bilbao
on the Channel Ferry. One look at the white caps blowing off the
scudding waves and I knew we were in for a queasy crossing. Thirty-six hours lying flat on my back below deck with my stomach being
tossed and rolled from one side to the other was nothing I looked
forward to. Small price to pay in exchange for four weeks in heaven
that for me was Ruesga, I tried convincing myself. But memories of
three eternal weeks of throwing up on the voyage to England from
India when I was seven year's old persisted.

I passed the hours on my bunk focused on all the things I hoped to do. We'd only ever seen Ruesga when green and gold dressed her hillsides and the village teemed with cows and people. I gave up trying to picture her fields denuded and dull. I could almost see Alejandro, Ignacio and La Madre huddled by the oven's open hearth in the kitchen; she, in her permanent shroud of black clothing and silver halo of hair, just staring, staring, rekindling memories from the flickering flames; and he, her son, running next year's crop cycle through his mind, all the while his fingers steadily working lengths of willow into a new basket for his mother for collecting eggs.

I turned my mind to cheerful things. No swimming. No harvest. This visit would be different for sure. We might finally get to see places like the roman bullring in Palencia, the church carved from one rock in Ollieros, perhaps even drive as far as Burgos and see the famed paintings in the Cathederal... My mind ran a mental list. Eight am, not long now. I checked the time and as I did, the ship's engines cut and the excited calls of the dockers announced our arrival in Bilbao.

We disembarked into another world, a world of sun and blue sky, which even the smoke-blackened buildings of the industrial city couldn't dim.

"Let's head for the hills." Ed said pressing his foot on the accelerator.

Half an hour later where the suburbs thinned to semi country, Ed slowed to a stop in front of a small roadside bar.

"Time for a celebratory glass of something, don't you agree boys? Let's see who'll be first to pick out the first swearword to prove we're actually here. So, quiet now, don't say a thing and let on we're not Spanish."

"*Dos cafés, sol y sombre, dos limomadas, y dos paquetes de pipas,*" Ed ordered our drinks casually at the bar as if he were a local.

We'd forgotten Spaniards didn't just speak in bars, they bellowed. In less than five minutes we began to giggle.

"*Maricon,*" Miles whispered hoarsely.

"*Coño. Me cargo. Jodere. Hostia...*"

In Castilian it seemed every sentence contained a graphic word.

Back in the car, we headed inland to the lower slopes and began the twisting climb towards the pass.

"Wow. Did you see that? The sign says, SNOW CHAINS RE-QUIRED," I exclaimed.

"Better check it out," Ed agreed pulling into a garage looking up at the sky. "The storm can't be too serious, after all this is April. Hopefully we can carry on. The garage people never said we shouldn't."

For the best part of an hour, the chains hampered our progress causing our Mini to lurch uncomfortably. A worrying line of darkening grey hovered ominously along the mountain range ahead.

"Now what," Ed cursed, braking. "We'll never get there at this pace."

Ahead, a string of lorries grinding up the steep grade forced us to a crawl. The first flakes hit our windscreen just as we topped the pass. Visibility dropped, but not alarmingly.

"Thank goodness for the red tail lights of those lorries," Ed said peering through the windscreen.

"According to the map we follow the lake for about twenty miles to Reinosa on the far side. Hurrah. From there it's less than an hour to Ruesga." I attempted to sound cheerful, "Hey boys, keep a look out for the right turn."

The minute we turned off, I knew we'd made a mistake. The lorries gone, headed East on the main road to Madrid, we were suddenly alone in a white, featureless world. Within minutes the snow fell so thickly, Ed was forced to open the window and use his hand to clear a patch in the windscreen to see where to steer. Should we go back? Keep going forwards? There was no way to know. We barely limped five miles when the mini slithered to a stop. Ahead, not moving, two tail lights, red, barely visible blocked our way.

"What the hell?" Ed jumped from the car and hammered on the window of the stalled vehicle.

"Are you OK? Are you OK?" He tapped the frosted glass urgently.

Blue-lipped from the cold, huddled together inside, two men stammered they'd been stuck in the snow for hours. Unable to move forward or turn around, neither their or our car was going anywhere.

Ed and the stronger of the two men, Jorge, hauled his companion, Mario, out of their car and half carried him to ours. Shivering uncontrollably, I could see he was in a bad way. I grabbed two of our sleeping bags and spread one over him and the other over the boys.

"Drink this," I commanded Mario handing him a thermos with the dregs of our coffee.

"The only way out of this is for two of us to go for help," Ed and Jorge decided.

As they passed the front bumper of the mini, the two of them vanished, swallowed by the white-out and descending dark. We were alone. Abandoned. Waves of fear prickled my skin. My toes felt numb. Heavy silence blanketed the car. The world beyond disappeared.

"Don't panic. Don't panic," I told myself struggling to appear calm. Oh, but I was scared. My thoughts ran riot. We'd die. We'd become hypothermic. Freeze to death. No one would ever find us. What to do when the petrol ran out and we had no heating? I pulled myself together. I had to. For the sake of my boys. It's up to me to keep us safe. I mentally checked...sleeping bags, yes, we could keep warm for a bit. Food? A couple of chocolate bars, a packet of digestive biscuits, water, a bottle of water. Divided by, say two days, it would last...

Then in mid calculation, a miracle. The shadowy figures of Ed and two men loomed towards us. A third? Where did he come from? But Ed was back, that's all I knew. I wanted to cry.

"We're going to be fine," I heard Ed shout. "The road patrol..."

The rest of his words whirled incomprehensibly. Ed told me later that ten minutes after leaving us, he and Jorge spotted the hazy taillights of a truck in the swirling blizzard turning around and about to drive away.

Stop. Stop, Ed broke into a run, he continued, and banged on the retreating vehicle's side door with all his might calling for it to stop. I could hear the relief in his voice as he relived the miracle, (or the divine intervention, to my mind) that the only vehicle still out there in the storm should be the road patrol. No-one could possibly be on the road ahead of them, the patrol men decided, and were actually in mid-turn to head back to their base when they heard Ed's pounding. A second later would have been a second too late. They'd have been gone.

Five days would pass before the main roads were cleared. Longer for this secondary road. In such cold and we would have surely died. I quashed the dreadful image of my children slowly freezing, the agony of witnessing their life slowly fade, or worse, leaving them to witness my death. I shook myself. By the grace of God, that hadn't happened. We'd been saved.

The patrol took command. With chains, effort and much shouting, their tow truck guided both vehicles to turn around and face the other direction. Slowly, slowly, slipping and sliding, Ed latched his sights onto their taillights and inched the seven miles behind them back to the main highway.

"All the roads are closed. We'll find you somewhere to stay." One patrol man got out of the truck and yelled into the car stopping in the deserted street of the first village we saw.

From the lit window of the first bar we came upon, startled faces peered at us in disbelief that we, anybody, should still be outside. Not a room was to be found in the whole village. Nor the second village either. Snow-covered abandoned lorries, cars and trucks littered the roadside. Finally, at the third village, *Cielo de Ventana*, Window of Heaven, the patrolmen negotiated one room with two narrow beds for the four of us above the second of the village's two bars.

"You've saved our lives," I thanked our saviors bursting into tears.

No matter frost covered the inside of the one window in the tiny room obliterating the street below us, we were safe. We were alive. We'd survived. Huddled together, wrapped in our sleeping bags, we relived our adventure till our terror abated, and our limbs thawed. In hindsight, that Ed and I could have so stupidly risked our lives is unfathomable.

That one roadside bar not only fed us hundred or so stranded refugees but lavishly with a seemingly endless supply of chicken, omelets, thick slices of ham, sausage, satisfying soups, cheese and newly baked bread. Wine, brandy, card games, dominoes, and bellowed conversation gave the crowded space a festive air. People stood or sat on the floor. Lorry drivers slept in shifts, we learned. Snow crept up and over the window panes darkening the daylight to an eerie glow, trapping us inside.

Miles recalls waking up the following morning to the glare of bright sunlight on snow that overnight had risen to just below our bedroom window. He has a clear image of seeing five or six men jump from the upper floor and shovel down to street level to un-block the front door, then dig a ten-foot deep channel across the buried square to the second bar. With nowhere else to play, Miles remembers running back and forth between the towering snow walls with the other kids.

Four nights and days passed. At last one lane was cleared. Lorries headed west were permitted to leave. Our turn came day five. We stuck to main roads. No way would we take the back route around the lake again even if it had been opened.

With one last look at Window of Heaven as we drove away, I mentally thanked those strangers for taking us in. If it wasn't for their generosity and kindness... I blocked the thought. What could have happened, hadn't. Thank you, God, I sighed

23

SPRING IN RUESGA

"Oh dear, I hope Mercedes hasn't given our rooms away. I feel terrible not having let her know," I kept repeating anxiously the nearer we came to Ruesga.

"Sorry. Sorry for not turning up when we said," I repeated guiltily. "We got trapped by a snowstorm in Cielo de Ventana for five days, and all the roads were closed."

"No problem You're here now, that's all that matters." Mercedes placidly waved away our apologies. "When I saw the heavy snow-clouds to the North, I knew you'd been held up and would get here when you could."

I studied her face. It was true, she really didn't seem bothered and accepted our late arrival with a philosophical shrug.

"Come in. I have your rooms ready." Overlapping a hand-knitted maroon cardigan across her chest, she grabbed the boys by the hand and pulled them inside from the bitter cold. "The bar's closed till May, so make yourselves comfortable in here. You'll have the kitchen to yourselves because I'll be eating with Juan and my family over in our other house where my mother-in-law lives."

Quickly shutting the outer door behind us and kicking off her muddy clogs, Mercedes opened the door into her kitchen.

"Sit. Sit," she indicated a couple of wooden chairs and stools pulled close to the fire crackling in the open hearth. "You'd like a glass of wine, I'm sure."

With that she disappeared into the dim and frigid back-parts of the bodega behind the shuttered bar.

I'd never been inside a Spanish kitchen in the two years we'd been visiting, not Alejandro's nor any friends, and had only briefly peaked into the Juanon's in passing during the summer, so was curious to see where she cooked.

Plain white tiles and a massive iron range spanned the entire back wall. Not a speck of soot in sight, its black cast iron surface gleamed silver-grey from years of scrubbing I assumed. As did the hanging pots and pans swinging from hooks. I was fascinated to see a small tap projecting from a narrow copper tank inset beside the hearth and part of the range. The sole source of hot water I realized with a start as I watched Mercedes top up its tank when she returned. I didn't envy her sweltering in a heatwave over the open range cooking our meals. I noticed a trivet set over a pile of hot ash to one side of the flames. On it something simmering in a lidded enamel pot filled the whole kitchen with the tantalizing aroma of oregano.

A faded wall calendar of a mountain meadow, and the flowered oil cloth covering the kitchen table added to the room's cozy warmth. She must have been in the middle of preparing a meal, for a mass of raw vegetables and pieces of chopped meat lay waiting beside the enamel pot she had ready on the table.

"*Bienvenidos*, I'm glad you made it," Mercedes smiled when she returned handing us each a small glass of *clarete*.

She bent taking a log from the woodpile and throwing it onto the fire. The only heat in the two-storied building, for the month we stayed at the Juanon, we ate our meals and clung to the fireside playing card games and dominoes whenever we weren't outside or shivering upstairs.

"Wow. Look Ed. See the *jamon*." I pointed to the side of meat hanging beside bunches of dry oregano and yellow flowered *Te*.

"It won't be cured for another two months at least," Mercedes remarked seeing us staring.

The occasional villager dropped by for a habitual pre-lunchtime glass of *vino*, and again before dark descended, turning Mercedes' kitchen to an informal gathering place to briefly exchange news before hunkering down for the night in their homes. Alejandro liked to pop by once milking was over, and we saw him and other village friends most days.

"To keep myself busy during the long winter evenings," Alejandro told us, "I weave baskets from the willow I've cut the previous year. I sell what we don't need to a man in Cervera."

"For you Isabel," he surprised me one day, handing me three.

"Me? All of them?" I took them overcome. "They're just beautiful."

Boat-shaped, the largest must have been almost two foot in length. Inside lay another smaller, and inside that, a round one the size of a wren's nest. I looked at his work hands, calloused, thick fingered, and pictured him sitting upstairs in the dark of his kitchen with his mother, the two of them silent around the stove, the crackle of fire, the swish of weaving, the sigh of satisfaction as another exquisite masterpiece lay finished.

Upstairs, downstairs, not a radiator or double pane of glass to be seen, frost crystals patterned our bedroom windows as it had in our room in Cielo de Ventana. I ran my fingernail and scratched a circle through the white before quickly pulling the shutters tight.

"*Brrr.* Torture," I shivered.

Jumping into bed, I buried myself beneath the heavy comforter trying to snuggle close enough to Ed to steal a little of his body-heat and thaw my feet.

By the morning our bed was so deliciously toasty-warm, it was almost too hot and I couldn't face leaving its cozy burrow. First, I pulled my clothes beneath the covers till the chill was off them, then dragged my clothing on before having the courage to leap from bed and run downstairs to the kitchen.

"The snow will be gone within the week," Mercedes predicted at breakfast.

"We'd better spend every second outdoors before the snow melts," we vowed.

"Who's for tobogganing today?" Ed asked.

The cerulean sky and brilliant sun we woke to that first morning stayed with us the month. Through the window, above the red roofs of the village, the surrounding mountains wore a cone of brilliant white. I'd been dropped overnight into a scenic advertisement for the Swiss Alps.

Though Ruesga itself had been mostly spared from the snow apart from a sprinkling, the ground was covered with a mush of icy mud and crisp frost edged every surface.

From the church tower the bell clanged ten.

Armed with metal trays from the bar, as excited as children, the four of us headed to the lake and up the mountain for the smooth slope below the pass above the mine.

Our cheeks flushed from the cold morning air and panting from exertion, we flopped flat in the powder to get back our breath. I watched a pair of dots soar overhead.

"Eagles," I gasped sitting up.

Yes, I was truly back in the Spain I loved.

"Remember last summer's rabbit picnic, boys? And Ulpiano and the hunter telling us to smell the earth, then digging out bottles of wine they'd buried?" It was difficult to believe how changed the valley looked buried under white, and with the lake's edge rimmed with frost.

Too chilly to sit for long, Ed rolled a handful of snow into a ball. A snow fight raged.

"One. Two. Three, race you." We whooped jumping for and onto our trays. Ten, twenty times, maybe more, we careened downhill kicking up soft clouds till we'd spent every ounce of energy.

No comida ever tasted so delicious as those Mercedes spooned onto our plates when we arrived back starving for lunch. Stews, chops, steaks, beans and cabbage, potatoes and hunks of crusty bread, sated our hunger.

Bundled up in gloves, scarves and heavy jackets, villagers clomped the streets with an awkward gait two inches above the mud and slush in three-pegged wooden clogs.

"My, how you've grown," we teased Alejandro seeing him clump towards us in a mud-spattered pair. No wonder he walked funny I noticed he still wore his canvas espadrills inside. Them.

A source of wonder to Alejandro, our striped tray-tracks we'd ploughed in the mountain side stayed frozen, visible weeks after the snow had mostly thawed. Alejandro pointed them out whenever we walked with him in the village.

"*Locos estrangeros,*" he shook his head amazed at us foreigners, grownups at that, playing like little children.

The snow gone, spring returned summoning orange and purple crocus to poke through the mountain grass. Life vibrated in every place one looked. I introduced my boys to mole hills, speckled robin's eggs, saffron stamens, and furled leaf buds in the hedgerows. We etched images and words on thin slabs of slate unearthed from the ground. We were family. Happy together.

"It's time to sow. The furrows are soft now and ready to receive my grain." Alejandro dropped the statement casually one evening. "I'm starting with the upper fields tomorrow."

Sensing his statement more of an unspoken invitation, he nodded happily when I begged if we could tag along. Sowing was the one missing cog in the harvest's cycle I'd not seen. I was excited.

The simplicity of sowing; a lone man, a sack, and seed, the rhythmic swing of step and hand as he strode the field and scattered was more beautiful a sight than I imagined. Grabbing a handful of grain from the sack slung from one shoulder, he opened his fingers and broadcast the grain in a gentle shower.

With no work for us to help with in the fields and more time to ourselves to explore further afield than in the summer, these cooler days were perfect to play tourist. We communed with stone saints in the cloisters of centuries old convents; marveled at the underground church carved from greenish rock in the small village of Olleros de Pisuerga.

A two hour's drive from Ruesga, one place on our list was the famed roman bull ring in Palencia still in use after a thousand years.

"In season," Ulpiano said, "...every seat for every bull fight is packed. I once saw the famous bullfighters, Paquiri and El Niño in the ring. What an honor."

Standing outside staring up at the towering structure, every stone looked as perfectly in place as the day slaves were thrown to the lions and wrestle not for their lives, but for a quick death. It was easy to imagine the roaring *Olé's* of the cheering spectators of then squished together thigh to thigh on the narrow benches in the more expensive, shady Sombre section of the arena, and Sol's cheaper seating in the full sun as they fanned themselves and quenching their thirst with wine from leather *botas* in the burning heat. Not much different from the bullfights of the present day, I thought guiltily recalling the shockingly unexpected excitement I felt watching the bull's fight to the death at the hands of the graceful matador. Ulpiano and Juanna had introduced us to our first bullfight when for three days the traveling bull ring magically appeared on the outskirts of Cervera the summer before.

Driving back, we were held up by the strangest of Easter parades in Valladolid's main street. In celebration of Semana Santa, an army of men in tall pointed caps and capes of swirling green looking for all the world as sinister as members of the Klu-klux clan, marched in solemn procession past the people lining the streets to an eerie drumbeat. Members of some brotherhood, I never did discover their relevance to Easter.

Back in Ruesga I wandered over to Manuella and Mariano's house one day. With little to call them outside, I'd barely caught sight of them since we'd arrived.

Bent over a hollowed trough carved from a massive oak, Manuella sloshed water over what turned out to be thighs of a newly slaughtered pig.

"This is how I make the jamon you like so much," she paused a moment wiping her face on her sleeve.

Feeling slightly squeamish, the boys and I peered to see what she'd been so vigorously scrubbing. "They've been soaking in salt-peter and a little honey for two days already, and now it's time to rinse off."

She bailed the water out with a mug then patted the haunches dry and stood.

"My back," she complained. "Fetch me that bowl one of you," she signaled the boys and sat on an upturned log adding, "I need to rest a minute."

We watched intrigued as she mixed up a startling orange/red paste.

"Black pepper, red chili and sweet pepper powder, cloves and a little salt. "Discourages flies from laying their eggs," she panted between slaps and rubs, slathering the mix into the flesh. "I'll turn it daily to ensure the paste is thoroughly soaked in. Then they're ready to hang over the cooking range and cure till next fall."

Manuella disappeared and returned with a few slices of last year's jamon for us to taste.

"*Dulce*. So good," I thanked her. Salty, sweet, we licked our lips.

"La Madre's making cheese tomorrow if you want to see how that's made," Manuella volunteered.

24

SOWING

"Tomorrow I sow. Tomorrow full moon." Alejandro dropped the information casually, almost coyly one evening. "I can feel the earth swelling to receive my grain. I'll seed my upper fields first."

I understood he spoke of earth's conception. The union of female, male. Was that the origin of the word Husbandry?

Sensing his statement more of an unspoken invitation, he nodded happily when I begged if we could tag along. Sowing was the one cog missing in the harvest's cycle I'd never witnessed. I'd seen old photographs, but never in real life. I was excited.

By the time we arrived at the barren field, the night's hoar frost still lay in the valleys between each furrow still lay etched with white.

I settled on a dry patch of earth on the field's edge to take in the scene re-enacted each spring for centuries glad for the sun's rays penetrating my jacket.

I pictured Alejandro as a lad observing, modeling his own movements on his father's.

In. Out. Swing. In. Out. Swing, the act more beautiful than I imagined, With the grace of a ballet super star, his right hand disappeared inside the sack slung over one shoulder, reappeared with a handful of grain and flung it evenly from his fanned fingers and thumb in a surprising rainbow.

The simplicity of it; a lone man, a sack, and seed, the rhythmic swing of step and hand. Transfixed by the beauty of Alejandro's retreating figure, I watched him work the length of the field's dark furrows. With slow, measured strides, he broadcast perfect arcs into the air assuring an even growth of golden grain harvest. I'd not questioned how the blocks of standing oats and barley grew so densely packed together they blocked my path as surely as a wall.

I thought of my own attempts to sprinkle the tiny lettuce and carrot seed in my London garden, the crowed clumps of growth and bald patches I created. The impatience I felt with my incompetence. My thoughts turned to Alejandro. His unruffled approach to life, the changing seasons and his part in the cycle of nature.

Peasant. Yes, in the true sense of the word, Alejandro was indeed a countryman, a man who lived off the land, a man whose knowledge held mysteries accumulated by generations. I'd never understand I felt ashamed for the times I'd sneered calling someone a peasant.

Pink cheeked from the sting of the early spring's crisp air, Anthony and Miles ran across the field excitedly each waving a slab of wafer-thin slate last year's ploughing had unearthed.

"Look stone age paper and pencils," they proudly held the images they'd scratched for me to examine. "For you, Mum. See, you can draw pictures with pointy stones."

They settled beside me at the edge of the field engrossed in their image-making. I patted their knees.

"Are you having fun, my darlings?"

Up one furrow, down the next, by midday Alejandro's sack was empty and his field impregnated. Fertile.

Ironic, I thought, when according to Ed, Alejandro had never lain with a woman.

That night as he lay in bed, Alejandro dreamed he was "fishing for frogs." For the one brief evening early fall that came round once a year when a man could thrust against the softness of a belly and grope between the thighs of any girl willing to be caught without question.

Blanketing the night, the air hung warm, heavy enough to obscure the "frogs" identities, he waited in the clump of willows along the river bank till the deepening shadows announced fishing could begin. Running, running with the pack of howling men, he probed the rustling undergrowth the on the scent of any giggling girl willing to be caught.

Even in his dream he never scored more than a fist between the legs. And when he tried to leap onto a girl's back to pin her down as he'd seen the Billy Goats do, he ended up clutching his groin from a vicious kick.

Dreaming over, Alejandro stirred, and mouth open rolled onto his back.

25

BIRTHING

Early one warm April evening while I was standing outside the Jua-non chatting to Mercedes outside her bar, Manuella came hurrying towards us.

"Bella is going into to labor," she panted. "We need you."

"Would you like me to come too, if I can be of help?" I asked.

"Later, yes. But best to let things settle first." Mercedes scurried off with Manuella to round up the other midwives.

From their separate houses they came, unhurried along the well-trodden dirt streets to Alejandro's home, Aurora, Marita, Rosal-ita and Mercedes each carrying a wooden stool, knitting needles and balls of colored wool in their apron pockets. Who knew how long they'd have to wait. Who knew how long the night, how many hours of labor and set off to tell Ed and the boys what was happening.

A little after sundown, I threw a cardigan over my shoulders and walked across the street to join the women.

Inside, the flare of a single ammonia gas lamp suspended from a low beam illuminated the women's faces. Disembodied, their black clothing almost indistinguishable from the dark shadows, the four women huddled quietly in the dim pool of lamplight to wait out Bella's impending labor. Looking up from their knitting the women nodded silently when I entered..

I gasped. A re-enactment of my own birth-story by the light of a hurricane lamp high in the Himalayas unfolded before my eyes.

"*Aqui*," Mercedes broke the silence as I pushed open the door. "Sit there. It will be a few hours yet."

Mercedes pointed to an extra stool. Pressing myself into the darkness and settling into the palpable vacuum of its silence, I shrank inside myself.

And as I did, I thought about the women's lives confined to this tiny spot on earth. Ruesga their only world, it was here the women had first taken breath, grown, married and themselves given birth. And was the place they would die and be buried. They sat so comfortably together, knitting away, not talking, I envied the bond they shared.

Every thought had long been spoken, every secret shared. A little village gossip, the changing seasons, nothing more exciting peppered their lives, they had no need for chatter. Aguilar de Campo's small town twenty-five miles away, was the outer limit to their world. Safe, familiar, content, they had no reason to stray beyond. I examined the women's faces. Aurora, Marita, Rosalita, and Mercedes. Scrubbed smooth, ruddy from a life outdoors, each face glowed with an inner light I rarely saw in my own reflection.

What if, like them, I had never traveled and had stayed in one place, would I accept my lot as readily as they did, or struggle to escape? India, England, Bahrain, Cyprus, India, Austria, Switzerland, France, Italy, and now Spain, I'd visited realms my Spanish friends never knew existed. What if, like them, I'd never uncovered the great universe hidden within the pages of books, would I have discovered an even greater kingdom within myself and in nature?

I recalled a conundrum. A community of frogs lived their whole lives inside a well, when one day a frog called down and told them of a far greater and more wonderful universe outside the confines of their well. Happy and contented with the familiar world they knew, they refused. Why would any of them want to leave their homes to explore the unknown, they answered.

I were one of these women and offered a choice, would I leave or stay like the well frogs?

Except Rosalita, Mercedes' cousin from Ventanilla, the next village up the valley, the other three were Ruesga born. Edging towards middle-age and no longer concerned with their looks, they kept their hair hidden beneath tightly knotted scarves. In the half-light it was easy to imagine them as girls when their dark tresses rippled free as the waters of the Rio Pisuerga.

But I'd seen another side of these normally friendly women that puzzled me. I'd watched them turn their backs on certain villagers as they waited together in the twice-daily bread line. I sensed a divisive undercurrent of hate that seemed so out of place in this idyllic rural village. It took me years to find out why Alejandro and his pals refused to patronize Maria's Upper bar. An ignorant outsider, I knew nothing of the cruel Civil War, nothing of the raw memories that still festered unforgotten and split the village into pro and anti-General Franco camps. Ed and I never again tried to persuade our friends in the Juanon to join us at Maria's.

I looked admiringly at Mercedes face, her calm demeanor, and understood why she was so respected in the village. Whatever their politics, everyone recognized Mercedes as their curandera, their wise woman, and relied on her remedies to cure them; which herb to take for what ailment, and what unpleasant treatment to endure. No matter what the illness, Mercedes injected the sick with penicillin with a needle so thick the very sight of it made me wince.

"It's beginning. Her waters broke." Mercedes interrupted my remembering.

I sat up instantly wide awake keen to witness birth as an observer.

Her first labor, Bella shifted, anxious, her moan loudening with the unfamiliar sensations wracking her body bringing back memories of my first son, Anthony's home birth.

I watched her arc and bend her head backwards, the whites of her eyes flare with fear. A wave of warmth rose from the neighboring stalls bringing sweet scents of hay, straw and grass. The overpowering smell of cow and cow patties intensified. As if aware, and in sympathy with Bella, the other cows, suddenly restless shifted in their stalls.

Mercedes and Rosalita, dropped their knitting needles and ran to her side. They slid their hands the length of Bella's silky hide clucking soothing encouragements. Marita rubbed the white curls between the curve of her horns with her palm and on down over her forehead and broad nose.

"There. There. Not long now," she encouraged.

Bella dribbled streaming strands of viscous spittle in her terror.

The women took turns playing midwife, petting, murmuring, remembering their own birth pains. Instinctively hands went to midriffs, each woman taking comfort from the gentle clang of wooden cowbells in the neighboring stalls, the sweet aroma of cud from the other cows, and the familiar sound of patties plopping onto stone.

When Alejandro brought his cows down from the upper pastures earlier that evening, Bella's distended belly told him her time had come. Milking over and the pails swinging safely out of reach from the feral cats, he hurried to fetch his sister, Manuella, from her house by the river, and tell her to go, go quickly and inform Mercedes.

Birthing was women's work, for the women who'd experienced childbirth. Not for spinsters or for the childless. Manuella, Alejandro's sister, married to Mariano, understood she was excluded.

No place for him and nothing to do but pass the time and wait, Alejandro climbed the wooden stairs and joined La Madre in their upstairs kitchen over the cowshed. Winter, summer, the old lady kept the enameled iron stove stoked. Selecting a log of roble, oak, Alejandro, tossed it expertly onto the embers. Lifting the lid of the blackened enamel pot, he sniffed hungry for the rabbit supper simmering on a trivet over the open fire.

"Manuella's looking for Mercedes," he explained to his mother.

"We'll eat when she gets back. Bella's gone into labor."

Pouring himself some wine, he drained the glass ignoring La Madre's pointed sighs, poured another, then sat to wait for Manuella. Silently counting the months on his fingers back to the time he put Bella to the bull. He nodded pleased the *pesetas* the bull's service cost him was about to pay off. Hoped it would be a cow not a bullock.

Bella, Alejandro smiled picturing his beauty, the prettiest of all the cows he owned. Her calf would be as beautiful he was certain. Perhaps the faded color of his upper grain-fields ripening in the August sun, he mused.

He sat up hearing Manuella's clogs clomp the stairs.

"Mercedes is on her way with three midwives," she panted dusting her hands before reaching for a flour-dusted, crusty ronda of bread for the table. Alejandro removed the glass chimney, lit the Hurricane lamp with a burning twig and waited for Manuella to fill his plate.

Downstairs in the byre below, where we women waited, the energy suddenly shifted. Palpable. Expectant. Mercedes lifted Bella's tail and thrust her free hand between the swollen lips of the cow's birth canal, felt around, withdrew her arm from Bella's vulva.

"Engaged," she announced wiping her arm dry on her apron and sat back on her stool.

Bella fretted. She stamped her hooves, bellowed, searching for relief as increasing contractions gripped her uterus.

The four women stood, never leaving Bella's side from that moment. A witness, I wished myself invisible. Intent on capturing the ancient scene unfolding before me a surprising burst of emotion rose in my throat as I watched how lovingly the women treated the cow.

Without being told, each woman busied with her separate tasks. Ruffling Bella's rump with her free hand, Mercedes, in charge, stood guard at the 'business' end. Rosilita, the youngest of the four and a new mother, gripped Bella's rope halter, placed her cheek against Bella's struggling to keep her still. Marita spread an armful of straw about Bella's legs. Aurora disappeared into the *quadro* returning with a brimming pail of water.

The calf's petite hooves and forelegs poked into the world, then its nose and head. It hung suspended for a moment as if testing the new environment, before the rest of its body slithered to the straw. Mercedes cleared a breathing hole in the birth sack to allow the calf to inhale its first gulp of air. Did the tiny creature call out, I can't recall? But I know Bella did. She lowed soft songs of mother-love to her calf and ran her tongue along her baby's back licking her new-born's damp coat to encourage her to stand.

"A girl," the women chorused.

"You can't milk a bullock. Alejandro will be pleased," they smiled at each other, their eyes fixed on the teetering calf as it struggled to balance.

First kneeling, then back legs straightened splayed, with one final effort, the calf quavered to its feet. Three times it fell before sum-moning the strength to try again.

"That's it little one. You're nearly up. Now for your reward."

Umbilical cord still dangling Mercedes put the calf to Bella's milk-distended udder.

"Come my precious. Suckle," she encouraged.

Tongue hollowed, wrapped tight around a dripping teat, greedy, the newborn's eyes rolled back in pleasure and obeyed.

All four women stepped away, wiped their hands, exchanged smiles, congratulatory nods, proud as if one of them had just deliv-ered. Rosalita quickly brushed away the wet tear trail trickling on her cheeks with the heel of her palm.

"You daft softie," Putting her arm around her, Mercedes laughed to hide a surge of emotion she couldn't own.

"Let's name her Estrella, for she was birthed by the light of stars."

They sighed nodding approvingly.

Aurora reached into a pail of salt she'd fetched from the bodega and rubbed it over the calf's' back.

"There, my beauty. Come on. Love your baby. The women stood back as Bella's coarse tongue rasped along the damp baby-curls of her newborn's back. Licking. Licking. Bonding.

"Now drink," Marita held a pail of water to Bella's lips.

With one long draught, the pail was dry. Marita left to return with another.

"They're both fine on their own now,"

"*Buenas Noches.* It went well." They nodded. "*Hasta mañana.*"

"Better not rouse Alejandro at this hour," they agreed.

Alejandro could wait till tomorrow.

I watched Mercedes and Aurora link arms and step into the night headed towards the Bar Juanon. Their faces florescent in the light of the Milky Way, shone. Marita took Rosalita's hand, kissed both her cheeks before separating. Stepping from the cloistered byre, I took a deep breath, inhaling the familiar scents I'd come to love. Heady wafts of cows, summer meadows, and peace, radiated from the earth.

A visitor, I didn't belong. A wave of loneliness saddened me. I lived in a city of paved streets with a man who drank too much. I wanted my life to be like theirs. Two months of heaven each summer were just not enough.

Unwashed, sprawled asleep in his under-vest, exuding manly odors of perspiration and grass, her husband grunted as Mercedes slipped in bed beside him and pulling at the rough homespun sheet and sheep's wool blanket and sighed.

A new life breathed on earth. A new life added. A cycle completed. Mercedes slid a hand across her husband's belly and closed her eyes.

26

BLOOD SAUSAGE AND CHEESE

The year we were snowed in and nearly died on the journey to Ruesga, by mid April a hint of green flushed Almonga's peak and the surrounding mountains. The snow line receded, and Ruesga's lanes ran slick with mud. Shuttered indoors from the inhospitable cold, Ruesga's buildings drooped as grey as the granite with which they'd been built.

Wrapped in shawls and winter jackets, people hurried by, faces downturned to avoid stepping in the rivulets of snowmelt running past their doors. Not till around mid-morning, when the sun finally burned off the frost, did anyone brave the elements and venture out. No point. With the earth frozen solid in the fields, any thought of farm work was out of the question. Apart from a brief courtesy call on La Madre, and the family's brief visit to welcome us the first evening in Mercedes' kitchen, we'd not seen sight of Alejandro or Igna-

211

cio. Sensibly, like La Madre, we, and they stayed tucked up at home.

The deserted village seemed somber without the splashes of scarlet, magenta and pink potted geraniums to decorate the houses. Unwelcoming even, the opposite of summer. No cart wheels creaked in the lane, no sound of cow bells or cheery housewives leaning from upstairs windows people-watching.

Like the villagers, we rose late, stayed buried like moles burrowed beneath our feather duvets. And only reluctantly emerged when hunger, or nature's call drove us shivering from our beds to huddle downstairs around the fire in Mercedes' kitchen for breakfast.

"You'll have to amuse yourselves this morning. I'm off to watch La Madre make cheese with the extra milk she's got. Two of her cows have calved," I announced to Ed and the boys over breakfast. "Bye darlings. Be good, okay? I'm off."

Anthony and Miles barely gave me a glance. They'd left the table and were down on their knees crouched beside the fire absorbed by the antics of the day-old litter of kittens crawling blindly over each other inside a cardboard box.

In the short time it took me to cross the street to La Madre's house, my cheeks had flushed pink with cold.

"*Holá. Aqui estoy,*" I called up the stairs praying her kitchen would be warm.

"*Ven. Passa,*" La Madre's shadowy form peered down at me from the landing.

Ready for action, apron on, and wooden spoon in hand, she waved me to come on up.

"We're just starting," she inclined her head towards her eldest son.

"Oh *holá,*" I disguised my surprise. I hadn't expected to find Ignacio helping his mother with work normally reserved for women.

"*Holá. Momento.*" Ignacio greeted briefly without taking his eyes off what he was doing. "*Dos. Tres.*" He continued aloud nodding each time he added a full measure of milk to a massive pan I could see heating on the range.

"*Quatro. Cinco. Seize litros. Ahora, finito,*" he concluded triumphantly before turning to smile in my direction. "Couldn't stop. Sorry."

La Madre had turned to an ogre. "*Levanté. Anadi. Filtré.* Do this,

212

not that. Stir. No slowly, now faster. Simmer. Simmer. It mustn't boil."

I'd always thought her so placid, bird-like even, never dreaming she could turn into the controlling taskmaster she became that day. On and on, her constant stream of orders pummeled her son.

I looked over at Ignacio. If being bossed about as a grown man bothered him, his expression never changed. He carried on his own way doing what he was doing and allowing La Madre's orders to crackle harmlessly over his head. I would have lost it if it had been me.

"It's important to keep it at a simmer," Ignacio gently explained, ignoring her as the caldron of milk began to steam and skin over.

"Careful. Careful. Don't let it boil. You've six liters there," his mother snapped peering into the pan.

I wonder if she'd have softened the way she spoke to him if she'd known he, Ignacio, her firstborn, would be dead and buried before the same time the following year.

Holding up a yellowed chicken's gall bladder the size of a pea for me to see, La Madre dropped it into the milk.

"Stir. Stir. Don't stop Ignacio," then turning to me added, "bile curdles the milk."

Was gall the natural form of the rennet I used to make junket, I wondered, as I watched uneven lumps separate from the thin grey liquid.

"See Isabel?" Ignacio said spooning the curd into a makeshift cheese cloth bag fastened over a bowl. "This is the time to add any herbs if you want."

Was I seeing right? I blinked twice to be sure. The bag he used was nothing but a sweat-discolored undervest with its arm and neck openings stitched closed.

"Now I squeeze out as much as I can," Ignacio twisted the bulging bundle as if it were a towel. "For later," he made the strangest face and raised his eyebrows indicating the liquid collecting in the bowl.

Mystified, I had no answer. A message clearly, though I hadn't the slightest idea what, and nodded as if I were a co-conspirator.

"*Vuelvo*, I'll be back," she disappeared. I could hear her rummaging about in the narrow upstairs storeroom at the top of the stairs. Returning with the largest sardine tin I'd ever seen, she placed it on the table and dusted it off. About five inches high with its top and bottom removed, it must have measured between twelve and fifteen inches in diameter. Ignacio pounded and pressed in the whole thing, bag and all, into the empty tin to set. It made the perfect cheese mold.

"Your turn, Madre," he said stepping aside.

Proud, as if she had made the cheese entirely on her own, La Madre elbowed him aside, and taking over rubbed both sides with a layer of coarse salt.

"Done," he wiped his hands on his trouser legs. "The sun does the rest."

Calmer now, the process was completed, La Madre trotted to the window sill and pushed the two geranium pots already there to one side. "There, that should be enough space."

Ignacio placed the cheese exactly where she'd pointed and weighted it down with a river stone.

"Good work, Mother, now rest." Taking her hand, he led her to the table.

Normally such a show off in the bar with his loud joke-telling and vulgar innuendos, I'd never thought of him as meek and kind. I liked him better after seeing the way he behaved towards the old lady. Was it because of his crippled arm he'd never married, I wondered? I'd heard the rumors, the stories of his liaisons, so it wasn't because he didn't like women, that he remained a bachelor.

Now all smiles, La Madre plumped down at the table patting the chair next to her for me to sit beside her.

"Come, Isabel. Now for our special treat," she said squeezing my thigh, affectionately.

As I settled beside her, I saw the hem of her skirt had ridden up above her kneesocks to reveal a yellowish white expanse of naked thigh. I don't know why, but their deathly pallor shocked me. I had a fleeting image of death. Hers? Ignacio's? I couldn't bear to look and turned quickly away.

"Wait your turn, my greedy kitty-cats," he gently scolded the two cats weaving and twirling round and around his legs. "Okay, I haven't forgotten. Here, puss, puss."

I watched him place a small saucer of whey on the floor.

"Now for ours," Ignacio dipped three bowls into the watery whey. "Liquid gold. *Salut*," he said downing the contents.

Wrapping her bony fingers tightly around her bowl, La Madre trembled slightly as she lifted it to her lips.

"*Bebe. Bebe*," La Madre ordered me to drink noticing my hesitation. "Go on."

I could hardly refuse with her looking at me. Controlling a grimace, I tentatively took the tiniest sip.

"You're right La Madre. It's delicious." I exclaimed, genuinely taken aback by the unexpected sweetness of the unappetizing looking fluid.

La Madre pulled herself to standing and headed to the top of the stairs.

"I'll let you know when the cheese is ready," she dismissed me politely.

The minute I got back to our room at the Juanon, I penciled out the recipe. Undervest. Neck and arm-holes openings sewed closed. Listing the ingredients and what I needed to make cheese I began to giggle.

"Now that, even I could make," I boasted to Ed later.

FARM CHEESE: Ruesga

Ingredients:
- 6 liters full cream milk. Unpasteurized.
- Chicken's gall bladder. Two.
- Salt, chives/herbs optional.
- 1 undervest. Washed. Neck and arm-holes sewed closed.
- Sardine tin. Large. Top and bottom removed.

Method:
- Bring milk to simmer.
- Add bile
- Stir till whey and curds separate
- Strain
- Add chopped chives, herbs to taste.
- Press curds into lined tin mold.
- Salt sides, leave for at least three weeks in fresh air to dry

One morning late summer, the year after Ignacio died, Ed, the boys and I popped into Alejandro's *quadro* as we often did, to find La Madre seated in her entry hall where the family preferred to sit during the summer months to keep cool. She liked us dropping by, not for any particular reason but to say Holá. Visiting was something all four of us enjoyed, sitting with La Madre and Alejandro, sometimes chatting, sometimes in comfortable silence.

Did they talk much of Ignacio since he'd died, I wondered, or had they buried his life and name along with him. I shivered remembering the dreadful story of his body being delivered home family when his family were expecting him alive.

The eighty-year-old sat huddled over a large earthenware bowl at her feet, breaking up small pieces of stale bread and tossing them in.

Wrapped in black, she seemed older that year, an ancient tortoise with her wrinkled skin and scarfed head bent almost to her chest, who'd popped outside her shell to check the outside world. Focused on her task, I wondered if she knew we watched her. As though she heard my thoughts, she looked up and stared at us sharply.

"I'm making *morcillia*, blood sausage," she addressed me reaching for a large yellow onion and slicing it into the mix.

Handfuls of cumin, thyme, cayenne, red and black ground pepper, then salt, and lumps of chopped pig fat followed. She sat back seeing Alejandro and Ed enter.

"Manuella's on her way," Alejandro told her.

At that moment her daughter appeared in the doorway leading a goat by one of its curved horns. The animal's soft, black curly hair glistened catching the light. Bleating plaintively, the creature hesitated uncertain of entering this human habitation, then trotted calmly across the flagstone beside Manuella to stand before La Madre. Leaning towards the animal, the old woman ran her fingers under its chin and down its throat, pinching, feeling for its thorax. Petting it, I thought, before I realized...Uh Oh...

Hearing a rhythmic rasping sound, I looked up to see the noise came from her son, Alejandro. Expressionless, he held a whetstone in one hand, and was drawing the blade of an evil-looking knife up, down with the other. Stopping every few strokes, he tested its sharpness with his thumb.

"I don't think we want to be here right now boys. Let's get the hell out," I ordered. "And now," I shouted fleeing with them and Ed outside to escape the killing scene about to play out.

Fifteen minutes, and the deed was done. The goat's empty carcass hung skinned and dripping from a beam onto the bread mix in the earthenware bowl making my stomach clench at the acrid smell of fresh blood. The two women up to their wrists in the gory ingredients, whisking and mixing to prevent clotting, reminded me of the witches in Shakespeare's Macbeth concocting their magical brew. But who was I to be squeamish? I ate meat after all, loved the taste of the dark *morcilla* sausage fried with a slice of bacon or served with kidney beans, and ate it for breakfast as often as I could. Half fascinated, half repulsed by the process, I forced myself to stay wondering if I could ever enjoy blood pudding again.

Festooned with a garland of sheep gut round his neck, Alejandro fetched and screwed a mincer tightly to the table edge, and handed the dried gut to La Madre. I fingered its texture. Similar to greaseproof or rice paper, dry, papery, almost transparent, nothing disgustingly intestinal about it remained. La Madre slipped an open end over the mincer's nozzle as if it were a condom, and held it firmly in place while Manuella wound its handle feeding in the morcilla-mix until coils of stuffed tubes lay on the table.

Perhaps because they were so familiar with the process, the three of them separated, twisted, stuffed the tubing and cut it to palatable sausage lengths, all without saying much. Though they never mentioned Ignacio, I imagine as they worked together, his empty chair loomed a constant reminder of his absence. I saw a family, a family I always dreamed of having but never had. Mother, daughter and son. I watched the three of them, envious of their obvious bond.

I scoured my mind for the times in England we shared anything like the same closeness, and found it harder than I thought. Mentally I listed the few times we did things together as a family, like Christmas, weekend walks in Richmond Park and along the river Thames, and occasional games of Monopoly around our dining room table, and that was it. One roof over four heads the only thing that united us. Not much else came to mind.

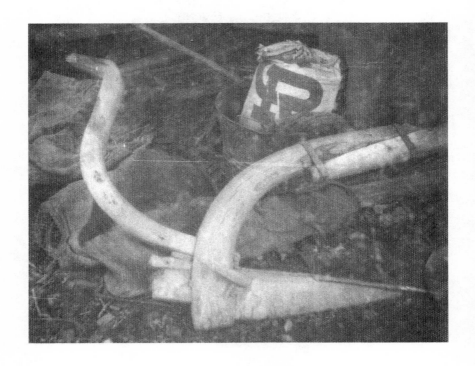

27

PLOUGH THE FIELDS AND SCATTER

I was back in England by the time the leaves fell. I'd never witnessed the season of Autumn, seen Alejandro plough his fields, but often played the scene in my head. I'd seen the neat line of Alejandro's ploughs along the wall of his barn, and learned his Papa had made two, and two he'd fashioned himself. The details I had to make up.

Alejandro rubbed his arms. Beside him on the riverbank the leaves of the Chestnut trees pattering yellow in the water caught his attention. He followed a leaf float lazily from a branch above him and ride the ripples past his boot.

"Tomorrow we must plough, Romera," Alejandro addressed his favorite cow.

Knee-deep in the shallows, her horns almost touching the surface, sucking long draughts of the Pisuerga as if to drain it, she rolled her eyes without interrupting her gulping.

Summer over, the signs were clear: clusters of sloes blued the hedgerows, sprays of rosehips sprinkled red. The rock-hard ground no longer accepted his or Romera's imprints. Alejandro stared at the clouds blown apart by a celestial being. They reminded him of tossed hay and pictured himself forking them into the loft.

Alejandro stood in the water's shallows below the bridge waiting while Romera siphoned the river down her throat staring idly into space. He noticed the storks were gone. The tangled stick-pile on the church tower lay silent and unoccupied. He wouldn't hear their clack of their beaks again till spring. He imagined how it would be to follow the sun's slant south to the edge of Spain and fly over a field of water and beyond it to another land.

Alejandro had never seen the sea, never understood a space filled with so much water. Lands existing beyond Spain's shores seemed too ridiculous to be true. Frowning slightly, he tussled with the fantasy.

"Come, Romera."

Without tugging her halter, she raised her head and plodded behind him muddying the drinking pool.

"Sleep well for tomorrow we plough," Alejandro whispered.

In the dim light of the barn opposite the milking stalls, Alejandro skirted his agricultural implements and felt his way to the far corner. The plough lay on the cobblestones beside his father's just where he'd left it, and beyond it his grandfather's carved more than fifty years earlier. A rotting icon, pockmarked by worms, the plough lay along the wall beneath a layer of dust. He paused, remembering his grandfather's hands, claw knuckles clasped about the handles, and his grandfather's face tunneled as the furrows he cut deep into the earth. Can't have been more than five or six, he reckoned.

"*Arar*, to plough. Romero," his father emphasized the syllables, the easier to learn them. "My Padre, your Grandpapa taught me the Roman way same as I'll teach you. You'll craft a beauty just as strong when you are older," he'd encouraged gently.

And Alejandro had watched his Papa's face soften as he ran his hands along the ancient shape unchanged since Roman times, its wood smoothed silky from a lifetime of handling.

He lost his first milk tooth he remembered, and how grown he felt the September his father called him and his crippled brother to accompany him and bring back the fallen oak tree he'd felled and left to season three years earlier for your plough, he'd said running his hand the length of its grain. "Plenty of heart-wood in this tree when the time comes."

Time came for Alejandro soon enough. His cheeks still smooth at seventeen, he slow-walked behind his father's coffin and grieved him into his grave, burned his father's clothes and boots and put away and moved his father's plough to the corner of the barn next his grandfather's. "Wouldn't be right to walk behind it," he'd confided to his brother as they lay in bed one night. "Might invite his ghost."

As *jefe* of the household, Alejandro determined he'd find his own way of doing things when time came to step into his father's shoes.

Picturing his father he swung his adze and shaped the plough the same way as he had been shown, and over the short days of winter pulled its form from the massive tree trunk. That be more than thirty year back, he mused.

Alejandro glanced at them. Three ploughs. Three generations linked. Grandfather to father, father to grandson, but he had no son on whom to pass this ancient skill. His plough would be the last. He ran his hands over the curve from the handles down to the shear. His palms ran smooth on the wood despite the tangle of cobwebs and dust and Madre's nagging tirade inside his head.

"You should have found a wife. Have thought of the Anton's family's future."

No time for *philosophizings*. Adding extra syllables, he'd silenced his guilt. Not my fault no girls wanted me.

It wasn't that he had never tried to snag one. Fifteen year back he snatched a kiss from La Sola's daughter, Eugena, when she walked over nice and friendly like, and sat with him in the high meadow one afternoon while he was up the mountain with the village cows. All went well until he pushed her over to her stomach, pinned her down and sunk his teeth into her neck like the drakes mated. She ran off yelling she was no *hija de puta,* and he was the son of a shit-pin-head-rooster.

Alejandro aimed a glob of spittle at the wall. The memory still grated. Ignacio's fault. *Womin' like a little rough and tumble,* he'd misled him.

Three arrow-shaped shears lay lined up on a gunnysack. Looking them over, he bent down and selected one to sharpen once he'd eaten.

Alejandro worked the whetstone along the arrow point till the blade was sharp enough to shave a cat's whiskers.

Should he start on his brother's, or his crop, in his, or his own upper field? He pushed his fingers beneath the hem of his *boina* and scratched his bald pate without exposing his baldness. He would let the field decide for him in the morning.

Called by the rooster's cock-a-doodling, the sun had barely crested the horizon when he rolled out of bed. Alejandro slumped down the stairs and stopped to pee on the cobbles like his cows before he began milking. Still sleepy, he pressed his forehead against the warm silk of Romera's hide, lulled by the squirt, squirt sound of milk hitting the pail as he squeezed the teats.

Milking over, he put his lips to Romera's neck sniffing the sweet grass smell of her. *Bella mio*, he murmured slapping her rump. She lifted her tail splashing green on the cobbles.

"*Voy arriba, Madre.* I'm ploughing our upper fields today."

The field strung ochre, an oblong strip of corn stubble above the village. Idle since summer it lay wedged between Aquilino's perfect stripes of furrowed field, and Juanillio's weed jumbled strip the other side. *Muerto*, he muttered. It wasn't something Alejandro dwelled on but its neglect reminded him his fields were destined for the same fate when age twisted his own limbs. Though fifteen years to the day had passed since he'd buried his father, as he trod the field alone without his papa, Alejandro felt his father hovering.

He wouldn't have noticed the crow if it hadn't opened its beak and called out to him. Caw, it croaked. Caw. Caw. Shiny-jet among the scarlet berries of the Rowan tree, its eyes followed Alejandro—daylong, boring holes into his back.

"*Cono*,"Alejandro swore. "Get your beady eyes off me." And as if the bird understood his annoyance, the damn crow hopped the field ahead guiding him as his father had. The intent of its stride, poke of its head, mourner's garb of death, and the hunch of its back planted the idea his *Padre* visited. Alejandro answered imaginary questions; *Si, Padre* I've scythed the hay, spread three cartloads of manure on the land, and laid the hedges for winter. *Si, Padre*. I tend to Madre, chop the wood and carry her pail.

He picked up a stone and hurled it. He aimed a second. The crow lifted into the air and set back down with a cackle of rasping complaints.

The plough shear beneath his hands sprang to life. He almost ran to keep up. The single shear uprooted the corn stubble parting the earth in a narrow furrow. Up, down when he turned the crow flew ahead to where the next groove should begin.

One furrow more and he would take a break on the field's upper edge. He could see the village from there. He fetched the cloth bundle from the back of the cart and patted Romera's rump. She swished her tail and continued chewing. He leaned against the wooden wheel, and lifting the *bota* gulped the wine without it touching his lips. Tangy with pitch, he savored its coolness. Sometimes he wished he chewed the cud as she did.

Alejandro swatted the cloud of midges swarming for the moisture in her eyes. Moving slowly, he led Romera back to work.

For almost the last time, though he didn't know it. Soon his fields would wither, untended and die. Franco would be dead before next season's ploughing, and his death would plunge Spain headlong into irrevocable change.

28

PORN POTATOES AND PLUMBING

EL GENERALISSIMO DEAD, CONGESTIVE HEART FAIL-
URE, headlines screamed around the world November 20th1975.

"That's it. The end," I moaned the first summer we drove into
Ruesga after Franco's death.

"Look. Can you believe it? Two other cars are parked outside the
Juanon," Ed exclaimed outraged.

Our village became ours alone no more, but by the end of the
week, we no longer stared at strangers, those trespassers cruising
through the village's narrow lane loaded with out-of-towners headed
for the lake. Luckily for us, if visitors stopped at all, they mostly fre-
quented Maria's comfortable Upper Bar.

Except for Sundays and Fiestas, when visitors from Cervera

swarmed the Juanon, we, the regulars, had the Juanon to ourselves. The lack of chairs and tables, our bellowed conversations and Alejandro's loud laughter was enough to scare any stranger away. An extension of our homes, our lives revolved round the Juanon, the place we liked to unwind and socialize. We carried on as we'd always done.

"Good riddance," Alejandro banged his hand on the bar. "No strangers welcome here."

"Same goes for our beach. Better not dispute our squatters rights." Ed joked.

We need not have worried. Put off by the uncomfortable strip of exposed land above the waterline, and its closeness to the road, people stayed well away from our swimming spot. The secret of its clear, deep water, diving rock and lone shade tree still rooted half submerged since the valley was first flooded stayed safe. Our beach stayed ours and our new friends from Madrid, Eduardo and his family, Leandro's cousins who swam and sunbathed with us most days.

The rowdy hoard of weekend picnickers congregated in the reedy shallows that ringed the meadow on the other side of the lake. Out of earshot, out of sight, we easily forgot anyone was there. Then campers arrived. One tent, then two. We'd glimpse them as we crossed the dam headed back down to the village. Smoke from their barbecues, kites and gamboling children playing ball. We didn't bother them. They didn't bother us.

"Have you noticed? The minders, those *Guardia* have gone." Ed remarked as we strolled through the village lane after a swim one day.

"Goodness. So, they have," I peered into Maria's Bar, their usual hang out.

It was true. After all the years we'd been going to Spain, the pair of patrolling Guardia de Civil embedded in the village had simply disappeared.

I remembered how scary they seemed to me with their uniforms and guns our first year in Ruesga.

"Take no notice. They're just lonely young conscripts from villages like Ruesga serving their two years," Mercedes explained.

Since then, like most of the villagers, I saw the pair of Guardia as poor kids whose only interest was to complete their duty and get back home as quickly as they could. Though they never exchanged a word with us, we nodded back whenever they did. It didn't take long before we learned to ignore the constant shadow of their green uniforms, shouldered rifles, and piercing watchful eyes as alert to every little movement, they peered from beneath strange, shiny-black, bat-wing headgear.

We became so used to the pair of Guardia wandering the lane, or skulking in a corner of Maria's Franco-friendly Upper Bar, we saw them as no more threatening than Ruesga's pair of nesting storks peering from the church tower.

In previous years, though our friends laughed and joked, I noticed they looked anxiously around if we let slip any remark that could be taken as politically subversive.

"Shh, *Cuidado. Voy al Cárcel.* You'll end up in prison," they used to whisper cautioning Ed, miming handcuffed wrists.

"So, no more shiny hats in every village then?" Ed remarked one evening during the first week.

"Nope. Gone for good," Ulpiano smiled. "Now we can say what the hell we please."

Alejandro and Ulpiano, their voices rising egged each-other on.

"… the priests…Those Franco-lovers…Yes, traitors to Spain… lining their pockets…demanding favors…guzzling Communion wine…the arrogant bastards…and worst of all, they demand sex from any new bride still childless. Celibate. Pah." Ulpiano spat his disgust.

I can't swear to it, but I could see they both believed the story to be true.

"I know it for a fact as it happened to a friend of my cousin's friend who hadn't been married a full year," Ulpiano looked grave. "The priest paid an unexpected visit knowing the husband was away working his fields. Returning home, he arrived to find an open umbrella hanging outside his front door. A warning sign to keep away. That the priest was there. Inside, upstairs fu**ing his young bride for not having conceived. Doing his duty. Giving her a child of God the dirty bugger. 'God's conjugal rights,' the priest smirked.

Ulpiano snorted. "Child of God indeed"

"Hmm. Surely that was rare," I exclaimed not really convinced.

"Nope. It's the custom round here."

"With Franco gone, most likely the new regime will stop all that," Ed switched topics, keen to hear Eduardo's and his friends' opinions on the changes needed to modernize Spain.

Money. Telephones. Plumbing. Automobiles. Electricity. Freedom of speech.

On and on. How their coming would improve their lives in a good way. Progress was necessary of course, but listening to their lengthy list of changes Ruesga as I loved would soon be no more. Enough. Enough. I wanted to shout.

Leaving the men, I walked slowly back to our tent aware of the night's timeless quiet, the heightened smells rising from the hedgerows, the heat of the lane's unpaved earth. I ached for my deserted meadow. I wanted to breathe, sit alone and search for stars streaking from the galaxy, for gaps their disappearance left in the sky. Nothing. The same confetti-spangled galaxy crammed the heavens as before. So maybe Ruesga's calm beauty would survive in an altered form in spite of...because of...

I thought about Mercedes. How change had caused the electrocution of our lovely friend. Our shock at first seeing her as she ran towards the car to welcome our arrival.

"Oh Mercedes," we exclaimed horrified. "Whatever happened?"

We couldn't help but stare. Her face. Her arms and legs. All of her. Albino-like, ugly snow-white blotches now stained her previously suntanned skin. Irreversible, changed forever. I saw her damage as an omen for Ruesga's improvements I knew were coming.

"*Nada. Nada. Compre frigidore. Tenemos electricidad ahora*, and Upè found me unconscious on the floor. I'm lucky to be alive...but my skin...the pigment...My skin is like this forever," she faltered. "I had just washed the floor in the bar when I stepped in there to put the milk into the fridge, you see. I didn't know it had a loose wire at the back that should have been grounded."

I turned to look. Prominent center stage, the fridge loomed from behind the bar. A bare light bulb dangled from the ceiling. Gone the hurricane lamps with their flaming ammonia gas, the hiss and flare of their green-blue light, I grown so used to. Electricity had arrived. Plumbing water too. It seemed every family decided to upgrade their homes and install bathrooms, so grand they were ridiculously out of place in their village homes.

"You've got a bidet?" I exclaimed amazed when Alejandro pushed open the door to usher Ed and I in to what used to be a store room off the entry hall.

"*Si. Si. El hombre* told us we should have one like our neighbors," Alejandro beamed.

A *bidet?* I secretly cursed the opportunistic salesman for pushing my friend to buy something he'd likely never use. Plain white porcelain tiles covered every inch of the ancient rough-cut stone. Ceiling, floor and all four walls. I made out the rain shower-head over a drain in the floor, the bathtub, basin and the *bidet*.

"I don't have to go outside to pump water any more now we've got a tap upstairs in the kitchen for La Madre." Alejandro's words spurted from his mouth in his excitement when we first met up with him that evening of summer '76.

"It rains like this on my back," he demonstrated wriggling his fingers.

Bending forward from the waist, arching his back, he hunched his shoulders awkwardly with his elbows bent like wings, and waggled in perfect imitation of a duck dancing in the rain. Smiling, leaning forward, he arched his back again. Imagining.

Already abandoned to a barrel and flagons of wine, a basket of onions, a sack of potatoes, flour and storage tubs of cheese, chorizo and varieties of sausage swimming in oil, it was obvious his bathroom had become a shrine. *Progress? Hmmn.*

I pictured La Madre sitting peaceably in the sun. Manuella brushing clean her mother's hair. Hair that in more than eighty years had never seen water. The convenient squares of newspaper hanging in the cowshed when I peed there beside the cows and wondered how much their lives had really changed for the better since Franco's iron control ended.

Some, I never imagined. Some, like watching porn, thankfully a one off.

"Porn. They're watching blue films," I whispered disbelievingly elbowing Ed.

I don't remember why Alejandro was not with us, or why we chose to take our evening drink in the Upper bar that particular evening, but when we entered, I remember Maria not welcoming us with her usual effusiveness. Shifty, is how I describe the way she looked as roars of coarse laughter exploded from behind a blanket strung to seal off half the bar.

"What's going on?" Ed questioned. "Where is everybody?"

"No. Don't go in there," Maria barred our way. "They're only showing a film someone loaned my husband."

"Can't we see it too?" He begged.

"No. No. Please." She vigorously shook her head.

The gales and cackles too much to ignore, the minute she left to bring us our tapas, we lifted a corner of the blanket and sneaked a peep over the crowd of heads packed into the darkened smoked filled space. Grainy images flashed from the projector across the far wall.

Hysterically pointing to the screen, the audience shrieked at what they saw as a comedy unrolling on the screen. Crude in its detail, acts they imagined reserved for farmyard animals, and the annual putting-of-the-bull-to-the-cows, they now witnessed enacted by humans dressed in nothing but jewel-studded dog collars.

"Look its mostly women in there," Ed whispered.

"Can't be," I muttered, but he was right.

Widows, married, old and young, cried with laughter slapping their thighs, and clutched each other to stop from falling off their chairs.

"I'm off," I nudged Ed.

The half-minute we stayed was way too long. We fled outside to gulp in the pristine air, wanting the foul taste gone.

"Well, if showing filth is an example of Spain stepping into the twentieth century, I'm speechless." I shook my head to loosen the images from my mind. "Did you see all those toothless old women there? Augustina? Theodora? Un-real."

Rubbing my arms and shivering in the evening's chill, I scurried beside Ed to our tent at the far end of the village. His arm around me, we gazed in silence at the Almonga Mountain outlined above the meadow and followed Venus slowly moving across the sky. At least she hadn't changed.

To Ed's and my relief, wooden carts still rolled slowly through the village. Alejandro's family still stopped work for merienda in the upper fields when we helped harvest his oats. Ignoring cars, their occupants' impatient hoots and yells, cows and goats still wandered the village lane blocking the way till they decided to move. Ripening fields of oats still colored the hillsides, and *la Era* hummed as every August with families threshing and raking. I was happy to see the younger women and girls wearing cut-off jeans and sleeveless blouses for the first time with their hair, like the dress code, loosened. The young men too, more relaxed, rolled their trouser-legs up and exposed their knees in the fields while they raked and scythed. Ed followed their example despite the jeers of Alejandro and his pals, who like the older men and married women still kept their bodies modestly encased in the shapeless black they'd worn all their lives.

At the beginning of this Franco-less era, the villagers harvested the old way as they always had. Our summer passed as magically as before. Until one day....

...a tractor chugged noisily past Ed and I as we headed for *la Era*.

"*Holá. Holá*," the driver waved.

"Look," Ed exclaimed. "That's Nano's tractor and Alejandro with him. I wonder what's happened to the cows?"

"*Nano dice su tractor* can pull several sledges at once and *terminado el trilliando en medio tiempo*." Alejandro didn't sound convinced that the contraption would really cut the time in half.

We stood and watched them struggle to hitch not one, but three sledges together behind the tractor to form an ungainly triangle, then dump a couple of heavy rocks on the first two to weight them down.

"Now you Alejandro. Sit there on the third." Nano directed.

"*Listo*? Hold tight." El Furia jumped onto the driver's metal seat and roared the engine into action. "*Anda. Anda*," he yelled dragging the unwieldy contraption forward.

No wonder people called Nano El Furia.

Belching exhaust, first slowly, then faster and faster at an increasing dizzying speed, Nano circled the *corona* of grain and burst happily into song.

"Wow. Just look at Alejandro, poor, miserable bugger," Ed bellowed over the noise.

Eyes scrunched half closed, nose blackened from breathing stinking diesel fumes, his face and clothes already coated with blowing dust and chaff, constantly tipping over, Alejandro struggled to keep his balance.

One hour. Two, Alejandro stuck out his torture before the oats lay threshed and ready for us to scrape into a new monton. Maybe threshing by tractor saved time, but was the gain of that single hour worth the cost of such misery?

"If that's an improvement, well…he can keep it," Ed and I fled in disgust.

I pictured last year's Era with its plodding gentle cows and circling threshing sledges hissing past without ever stirring a speck of dust, the ripe scent of crushed grain, the heady aroma of sweet of clover.

"Remember how we laughed when Miles was told to catch the cow shit, and we kept falling off the scraper into the giant montons, of grain? And…and…"

Had we witnessed a threshing by cow-drawn sledges for the last time. A method of harvesting oats first described before the birth of Christ? Depressed, I prayed the traditional ways would last.

My spirits lifted the following day when I saw Alejandro hitch Tesuga and Romera to their yoke, lead them towards *la Era*, and revert to threshing with his cows as he always had. Peace descended for the remainder of the season and forever, I hoped.

But it was not to be. The following year, Ruesga's lower fields crawled with the infernal tractor-machines. And like a plague of bees' incessant buzzing fingered every corner of the village, for once one family owned a tractor, every family wanted a similar new-fangled machine.

Not to till and plant the land with oats, but to harvest potatoes.

"*Papas. Papas.* Did you hear…? Did you hear…? The Juanon shimmered with gossip those evenings, late summer after harvest festival had passed. "I heard it today from those government men who were up at Maria's bar."

"Any family who converts their land to grow potatoes instead of oats, the State will pay massive hundreds of *pesetas* a bushel. Cash."

The first year, two families fell for the bait, converted their land to grow potatoes and earned more money than they, and any villager, had ever dreamed of. That fall, all but Aquilino's, the Roldans, Antons, every family in Ruesga abandoned their upper fields, ploughed deep furrows through their lower meadowland, and planted the new crop. Thank God we'd already back in England when, like a plague of bees with their incessant buzzing, Ruesga's lower fields swarmed with the infernal machines. Once one family owned a tractor, every family just had to have one. All but Aquilino's, every other family, the Roldans, Antons, Franciscos, every household in Ruesga abandoned their upper fields, ploughed deep furrows through their lower meadowland, and planted the new crop. The seed potatoes fattened, spread their spidery roots beneath the sod and in early summer yielded up their bounty.

"There's a potato glut. We can only pay two *pesetas* a bushel this year," the government officials informed Alejandro and the other villagers.

Alejandro led us to a shed and swung the door wide. Taking a step back, Ed and I gasped. Potatoes. Potatoes. Tons and Tons. Floor to ceiling. Nightmarish. Ghostly pale. Translucent tendrils stretched eerily towards us in the doorway where we stood, searching for the light, for life. It's a sight I'll never forget.

"*Cabrónes*. They can *jodere* themselves," Alejandro eyes flamed with anger as he exploded.

"I'm not selling those *hijos de putas* a single potato. I'd rather dump the lot of them in the Pisuerga River than accept their measly *pesetas*."

And so, he did. Alejandro was not the only one. The villagers banded together refusing to sell. Every last family threw the every potato to their pigs or into the river. The government hadn't bargained for Ruesga's Spanish pride.

29

CAMPO MUERTO

"You are already living the life of a millionaire without having to earn a *peseta*." Ed paused, allowing his point to sink in. Ever since the first two villagers gave up growing oats and earned all that money from potatoes, he and Alejandro argued endlessly over many a glass of *clarete*. "So why change to growing potatoes for an risky Government pay-out?"

"Don't you get it?" Ed prodded. "You own your land, both your and Mariano's houses, grow all the vegetables you need, and can choose when or not to work, while we, and everyone we know back home have to struggle to live half as well as you do."

Now that most houses had installed electricity and running water, beyond a few modern comforts like television, a fridge, a couple of upholstered chairs and perhaps double glazing, I couldn't think of much else that would improve my friends' lives.

"What would you do all day, Alejandro if you weren't working? Get fat and pale skinned from sitting around like you told me you do in winter?" I persisted.

Not actually admitting it aloud, of course Alejandro recognized the truth of what we said, and pushing back his *boña* revealing the whitest, shiniest bald pate, smiled enigmatically.

"Watch out Alejandro," Ulpiano and Leandro teasingly snatched at his beret exposing his polished dome. "Look the moon's already got in your head. Better cover it up quick."

Though we laughed with them, inside I sagged. Would I never again work on *la Era*, ride a threshing sledge? The thought of Ruesga's surrounding hills no longer signaling the seasons with its changing colors was too painful to think about. I already mourned my loss. No swaying cart to plod behind to reach the upper fields; no happy *merienda* with the family stretched together in a patch of shade after a hard afternoon's work.

Did Alejandro listen? Why should he? Like his other friends, seduced by the thought of money, he gave up his oats and switched crops.

I sighed. Village life would not ever be the same again. All that I loved gone forever. I turned my back on the old ways and with Ruesga, faced her coming of age.

"*Campo muerto*," Alejandro shook his head pointing to the shorn and abandoned, now arid hillside where as recently as two summers back, we helped Alejandro's family gather the golden harvest.

And indeed, the fields were—dead. Alejandro mourned each by name as tenderly as if he'd lost a friend. Mariposa, Luna, Laura, Lupe, Flora. Never more to bear another crop, his fields withered, barren. I wanted to weep. Now overgrown, the web of lanes to the upper slopes above the village carved from the rocky earth generations back, and the fields themselves, lay invisible beneath the encroaching tangle of thorny blackberries and thistles. Impassable, the boys and I were forced to circuit miles out of the way to reach the Almonga's steep slopes whenever we wanted to search for herbs or hike for the pure joy of being closer to the sky.

Once machines took over and I gave up working on the land, it was as if a crater opened in my life. Empty of her herds of cows, flocks of goats and sheep, rooting pigs, Ruesga became as an abandoned house stripped of its contents. *La Era* became no fun for me anymore with its cows and sledges gone, and tractors chugged instead.

Angrily, I blame that Government subsidy for the final destruction of Ruesga's rural paradise. Those agricultural lackeys who engineered the dishonest, tempting potato-growing deal, those city officials who lured the villagers with riches they knew they'd never have to pay out. Two seasons later, once the fields converted, and families became no longer self-sufficient, Ruesga was no longer theirs, beholden to whatever price per bushel the Government chose.

Autumn crept over the mountaintops from the coast to forecast the coming of early frost. Too late to reclaim the land, Ruesgas' families dug and stored the winter vegetables they needed, prepared the meadowland for the following spring and shopped in Cervera for any goods they lacked.

The newness of money struck me the time we drove Alejandro to the miller's yard to buy his annual sack of flour. Pulling a fistful of *pesetas* from his trouser pocket, I watched him stare at the paper clutched in his palm as instead of bartering as he'd done all his life, the miller took what coins and notes were owed in exchange for a sack of flour. I thought back wistfully to the last day we harvested, how proudly Alejandro surveyed his sixteen sacks, and counted, then recounted, the sum total of the year's hard labor that would keep the Antons' two households in flour for a year as it had for generations. One sack of golden grain in payment to mill the flour, one sack for a year's supply for La Madre and Manuella to cook, make their bread with, and supply enough grain to feed their pigs and chickens.

"Those sixteen sacks are all your family need to survive on for a whole year?" I remembered my astonishment. My guilty flashback to the cans and bags and frozen goods crammed into my London cupboards.

"Don't you miss growing your own grain?" I asked Alejandro as we waited to be served in the Florida Bar where Ed had taken him to see the first, and only television in town.

Too absorbed, not listening, he shook his head eyes fixed on the blurry grey images.

I just made out a plumed circus horse prancing around an arena, a dancing ballerina balanced on its back.

"*Caballo. Veo un caballo*," Alejandro exclaimed waving his wine glass at the horse. "*Pero*, I don't understand how that lady with the umbrella is walking in the air?"

"What do you mean?" I countered before I could stop myself. I tried thinking back to seeing my very first film, Bambi seeing and wondering why I couldn't feel the flames when the fire roared through the forest.

Looking back at the grainy television screen trying to see the images through Alejandro's eyes, I realized that unless you knew a tightrope stretched high across the circus ring, the trapeze artist did appear to be jumping and landing on nothing but thin air.

"Wow," I commented later to Ed. "That's like Mercedes not understanding the reflection of her church in the water. Remember her puzzlement when we handed her a photo of the village where she was born, and her turning it round and around? 'I can see it's my church, and the village pond, she said. 'But why are there two churches and one's upside down?' Remember how shocked we were."

One hot, August morning after a morning's shopping, weighed down with three day's food, hot and thirsty, I took the boys for a lemonade at a family bar in the center of town to wait for Ed. Known for its cakes and ice cream the Florida was the only place I'd seen women and children. With its large windows and spacious saloon, mirrored walls and pastry-filled display counters, frequent customers, Ed and I often took the boys there. Already crowded, I went to the bar.

"*Tres limonadas*," I smiled at the owner-bartender pointing to the table where Anthony and Miles sat.

Sweating in the heat, I flopped beside my children to wait. Five minutes I flagged a waiter and repeated our order. Nothing. Desperate, my thirst became all-consuming. Another five ticked by. I raised my voice just enough to see the bartender freeze. I realized he had no intention of serving me. Pushing back my chair, I strode to the bar, thumped the wood and shouted, "three lemonades," a third and then a fourth time. No longer able to ignore me, avoiding eye contact the bartender turned his head and shoved three bottles of Fanta across the bar—not the limonadas I ordered. He left my *pesetas* scattered on the bar, refused payment. Refused to touch my dirty money. Being deliberately insulted.

"We need to leave. Now," I hissed at Ed when he joined us.

Back in our village, I complained to Mercedes about how I'd been insulted.

"You went into the Florida Bar alone? Without Ed?" Mercedes gasped wagging her finger. "*Non. Non. Non.*"

"But they know I have a husband. We've been going there for nearly eleven years." I countered. "They're usually so friendly, and even give the children chicle-gum."

Still stuck in the old ways, unwittingly I'd trespassed a cultural barrier and tasted a little of the discrimination unaccompanied, married, single, women experienced daily. Not so modern after all.

"*Las dos solas*," Alejandro sniffed tapping his temples with a forefinger indicating we should wise up, keep well away from widowed Angelina, and Pilli whose husband ran off with a bartender ten years earlier making their morality questionable.

"*Putas*," he spat and Ed should watch out when he suggested offering to help them. Over the years, I'd seen them doing man's work in the fields every day, saw them fade a little each year destined to die lonely and too young. Angelina and Pilli. Mother. Daughter.

In Franco's world villages and towns of rural Picos de Europa were still on lock-down.

I don't know why I thought, with Franco gone, Spain would change overnight. And materially it had. Perhaps that explains Ed's stupid confession to his good friend.

"You know, Alejandro, Isabel and I are not actually legally married," he confided.

That evening in the dusk as the three of us, Ed, Alejandro and I were strolling to the Upper Bar as we usually did, a fist from the rear thrust roughly between my legs.

What the hell. He must be drunk, I thought batting Alejandro's hand away.

Undeterred, again, again, he forced his fist between my legs.

"How much for a *flin-flan?*" He whispered with a sneer moving so close I his hot breath blew against my ear. "*Vente pesetas?*"

Had the man gone crazy? I glared at him angrily, and yanking away his hand moved quickly to Ed's far side.

At last. The bar. Salvation. As we stepped into its circle of light, I grabbed Ed. "Alejandro keeps goosing me and won't stop. He even offered me twenty *pesetas* for a fuck," I muttered.

Wham. Before I knew what was happening, Ed slugged Alejandro in the face and knocked him reeling to the ground. *Wham.* Bare fists flying, a boxing match ensued. Ed yelling, Alejandro cursing, the long-time friends were out to kill one another. Astonished, half a dozen people rushed to separate the two and drag Ed away and into the bar. Alejandro vanished into the night headed for home.

Forever, it turned out. That was the last Ed and I saw of him. Alejandro never joined us for an evening drink again.

With a week to go before we left for England, Alejandro's absence loomed everywhere. Though no villager referred to the two men's falling out, and no-one behaved any differently towards Ed or me, I became uncomfortably conscious of people's curious glances.

True to our pattern, that Sunday, Ed and I treated Juanna and Ulpiano to a goodbye feast of seafood at the Penalabra in Cervera. Replete and happy, suddenly sad, we hugged each other promising we'd be back in Ruesga before they knew it.

A la proxima. Besos. Abrazos. Juanna and I dabbed our eyes, and wished the next ten months away and we could see each other again.

I hated leaving. That evening, our final till the following summer, wanting to be alone, I strolled to the dam for one last look at the lake.

The track curved steeply past Gusto's house before leveling out across the dam high above Ruesgas' red-tiled roofs, and overgrown Era. Turning my back, I leaned over the presa's massive grey, granite wall, and looked long and sadly at the flooded valley of water glinting in the evening light.

EPILOGUE
50 YEARS LATER

It hurt. Physically, as if I'd been stabbed in the heart, when twenty years after leaving Ruesga, I spotted a threshing sledge displayed in the window of an American Antique gallery.

If you only knew, if you only knew, I wanted to scream at the galleries' owners, can't you see it's a beautiful tool not just a decorative object of beauty.

FOR SALE. COFFEE TABLE. $1,500. Inanimate, robbed of its life force, its polished oak platform dulled, lay flint-side up under a slab of plate glass. Useless. Forgotten. Inevitable, I supposed, once Franco died taking Spain's ancient agricultural ways with him when he sprung Spain into the mechanical age.

Though it was not our intention to never return to Ruesga, or to leave our tent wrapped and stored forever in Mercedes' barn, how could we go back? Ed and Alejandro not speaking, no fields to work in, no harvest to gather, no cows, nor carts to ride in, somehow the next summer in Ruesga just never happened. Riddled with guilt, ashamed for so unexpectedly abandoning our Spanish families after they'd welcomed us into their lives, explanations seemed useless.

During the year Ed almost lived in the Pub drinking with his friends and became more and more abusive till I finally found the courage to pack all his belongings into my car and kick him out of my house.

Gone for good, Ed vanished from my life. I gave up my profession, my London home, emigrated to the great U,S of A and made a new life for myself in the wilds of New Mexico. There, I found David, a beautiful and kind man wanting to marry me, and began to write.

I mailed Christmas packages and photos to Ulpiano and Juanna and wrote them of my news, what the boys were doing, of my new marriage, and of their lives, and waited eagerly for their reply. When five or six years later, learning his lovely Juanna had died and he'd given up his Cervera home, I wept. I pushed Ruesga from my mind.

"I've moved to Santander to live with my niece, Pilli, in the Fishermans' Quarter," Ulpiano wrote. "I can see the sea from her house and I've built a shed at the end of the garden for my rabbits."

Laden with gifts, I took David, my American husband, to meet Ulpiano while we were in Spain. Injured two months before he retired, the coal mine refused him his pension forcing him to live on a pittance. Lost in a maze of streets, I turned a corner to find him anxiously waiting at the top of his street to guide us to his new home.

"*Aqui. Aqui,*" he waved frantic in case I couldn't see him.

"How I've missed you. And dear Juanna…I'm so sorry…" with tears running down our cheeks, we fell into each other's arms an grieved.

For fifty years, I stayed away from all my old friends in Ruesga. For fifty years I thumbed the photographs of our summers in my album, remembering, wishing, longing… silently thanking them for those eleven years that changed my attitudes and behavior forever. My children's too. Neither forgot the freedom of running where they chose and discovering the simple pleasures of country life, or the friendships they made.

Material wealth lost its value. Anthony and Miles revisited Ruesga again and again, traveled the world and no longer saw Britain as the center of the universe.

And when Miles married, he took his wife and children to introduce them to the village and his Spanish friends. Then in mid-career he and his wife gave up their safe careers, sold their house, and moved from London's restricting suburbs with their children to build new lives in a rundown farmhouse in the remote mountains of France. *Si. Non. Bonjour. Merci.* Like us with Spanish our first summer in Ruesga, their French was negligible.

Because of Spain, Anthony also realized he had a choice in life… to lip read, speak and be comfortable in the world of both the hearing and deaf rather than be channeled into the isolated world of sign language like most deaf people. Like his brother, like me, like Ed, Anthony picked up Spanish one word at a time. Ven, the villagers mouthed beckoning. Holá. Gracias, Donde? They gestured. Just like the rest of us, he quickly acquired an impressive list of nouns and verbs after just one summer in Ruesga.

To celebrate my eightieth, my Parkinson-suffering husband and I flew to France for a four-day friends and family party. As a treat, my daughter-in-law and Miles took us to Spain and a day's visit to Ruesga.

Would they remember me? Hold a grudge? Accept my new husband? Would I recognize anyone? Would my friends be dead? Would I hate seeing the village if it was changed? *Worry, worry, worry.* Driving over the bridge, I felt almost sick. There the Church, there the Almonga, there the row of houses, we passed Alejandro's house and pulled to a stop outside the Juanon. *PLATAS TYPICAS* read the sign over the door.

"Isabel," Upe and Juanco called out my name in disbelief as I emerged from the car. Next minute, smothered in their arms I was weeping with them in joy and being hugged so hard I might break in half.

"Juanco and I now own and run the Juanon," Mercedes' daughter,

Upe, her son Juanco, told me, pulling me inside the bar/restaurant where once Juan's hay barns stood. "Javi too. He lives here with his wife and children. Visitors come from all over to eat here now. *Ven. Ven. Sentarse. Sentarse.*" Tears and words spilling, they sat me down.

"You'll all eat with us. No question." Upe retuned with wine and saucers of tapas before vanishing towards the kitchen. She sounded and looked so like her Mother, as if I talked with Mercedes herself.

A life line to the past, his muscular hands clamped over mine, Juanco sat close as if to stop me from disappearing before we had time to catch up on the last five decades since I'd driven away from Ruesga. He looked so like his father, Upe so like her mother in her mannerisms, I had to keep reminding myself it was not Juan and Mercedes I sat with, but their children.

Stirred by memories, I wandered up Ruesga's tiny village lane to Maria's, the Upper Bar, as I'd done so often all those summers ago.

Gone the cows, and sweet scent of grass, but otherwise Ruesga felt the same…no added buildings, no shop, no neon signs, apart from the tarmac now covering the dirt, and the neat new cottages and flower gardens of converted barns and haylofts.

I saw a man I didn't recognize, sharpening his scythe in his yard next to Mariano's and Manuella's house. I wanted to see if the tree log beehive still protruded from the upper wall. I stood sadly looking at their abandoned home, the collapsed roof now sagging on its tumbled walls. Searching for evidence of the old ways, maybe a threshing sledge, an abandoned winnowing machine, an old cow shoe I wandered onto *la Era.*

Goalposts stood where once montons of grain clustered, and a group of children chased a soccer ball instead of gathering the harvest as they would have done before, I heard no echo of its threshing past, saw no faint outline of a *corona* imprinted in the grass.

Leaving, I climbed the curving track to the lake to see again our diving rock, the lone tree still growing half in half out the sheet of water where my boys and swam almost every day. And from the presa's granite dam I gazed down at the village, and surrounding grass covered hills where Ruesga nestled. Contained beneath the same red sea of rooves, Ruesga looked as idyllic as it always had. And I realized, though things were not nor could never be as before, despite the changes, a calm I'd yearned to feel for fifty years swept over me. The spring returned to my step.

Over *comida*, back at the Juanon, I stared at the yoke, the hand-carved rake and fork, the framed photo decorating the dining room wall. The black and white image, I remembered taking with my Brownie Box camera caught my eye. Juan riding a threshing sledge, the pair of cows, half buried, ploughing through the sea of grain. Staring into the lens, Juan is smiling.

"See. All is well. Ruesga lives and has survived."

grain thresher, Anatolia, 19th century
Bosshards Gallery, Abiquiu, NM

Acknowledgments

Catherine Ferguson: artist, writer, poet, author of many books. Without your patient feedback, this version of the book could never have happened. Thank you dear friend for our shared weekly master class, I'm forever grateful.

Donna Brownell: designer, technical assistant, friend. But for you, storm-blown pages and jumbled photos would still lie scattered, disarrayed as autumn leaves. I can't thank you enough for the valuable hours you gave me to format the book into a readable form.

Then my two sons, Anthony and Miles, I thank you for being in my life and sharing my Spanish journey with me. Finally, Covid. I thank you for the gift of time, the two year's isolation the devastating pandemic forced on me.

Elizabeth Rose, born by the light of a hurricane lamp on the dining room table in the Himalayan foothills, India, now lives and works in Galisteo, New Mexico, USA. Since emigrating from England, though she had never written anything beyond a journal, in the fall of 2008 she joined the SouthWest Writers in Albuquerque to hone her craft. Since then, Elizabeth has received more than a dozen awards for her writing, and published four books before this present book about Spain. Next up: a collection of short stories, followed by *A Raj Baby Speaks*, an account of the not so glamorous life of a child born during the last years of the British Raj in India. Writing is her passion.

Also by E.P. Rose:

Poet Under A Soldier's Hat

portraits : poems

The Perfect Servant...nope

Ditty Dottie Ditties

CPSIA information can be obtained
at www.ICGtesting.com
Printed in the USA
JSHW020732081122
32800JS00003B/182